Christopher LOGUE'S

TRUE STORIES

Illustrated by
Bert
KITCHEN

SBN 233964967

I had no good reason for writing this book; but such considerations rarely deter authors.

The habit of clipping I learned from my father, and of re-writing stories I clipped, from a wish to emphasise the funnyness or the hopelessness I saw in the original reports and that, surely, the journalist who wrote them – with whom, by rights, I should share whatever royalties come my way – also saw, but had for professional reasons to overlook.

In deference to my publishers I have changed the proper names in one or two of the stories.

ACKNOWLEDGEMENTS

My chief debt is to the reporters, sub-editors, and editors who got the material into print in the first place, and my next to the members of the human and animal kingdom who acted out the stories told.

Thereafter, and at random, it is to the people who bothered to send me clippings I would otherwise never have seen: Simon Watson-Taylor, Michael Kinnear, Louis de Wet, George Melly, Xanthe Wakefield, Patrick Brangwyn, Tuli Kupfeberg, Hugo Claus, Alan Ginsberg, Philip Oakes, Jean Hart, Elizabeth Moore, Talitha Pol, Clive Goodwin, Rodger Smith, Fritz Spiegl, Christopher Game, Austryn Wainhouse, Jane Kennedy, Mira Coopman, Germano Facetti, J.E. Lawford, Nicholas Zvegintzov, I.R. Bloor, David Campbell, H.E. Green, P.M. Young, Edmund Sinclair, Peter Shipton, John Upton, A. Hunt, Joseph Hone, L.P. Weldon, Geoffrey Spencer, David Moreau, P. McComisky, J.B. Rushden, D. McKie, R.Q. Little, Mary K. Williams, Michael Collett, J.A. Twelves, Sukie Marlowe, Tom Sharratt, Eric Lysholm Christensen, R.N. Stow, John Singleton, Rodger Perry, John Doran, Penelope Gilliat, Jake McTigue, Andrew Ritchie, C.J. Britcher, Anthony Green, Keith Harrison, M. Brown, John Michel, T.R.D. Shaw, Keith Barnes, Michael Popham, Trevor Royle, Christopher W. Dix, D.E. Spilsbury, Jack Robinson, John Sinclair, Bill Glen, A.Z. Ranagly, M.J. Hosenball, Peter Jessop, Stephen Borcic, Ruth Conick, David Kilburn, Tom Neale, Barry Humphries, Christopher Grey, Paul Getty Jnr, Mike Harper, Christopher Robinson, Annabel Bartlett, Caroline Henton, N.E. Sarsfield, Malcolm Hall, Geoff Wilson, B.K. Atkinson, Mary Knopka, David Stedman, Carmilla Dinkel, Arthur Hill, Nicholas Luard, W.G. Broads, Jenny Bagley, R.A. Heaps, Simon Fairthorne, Julian Taylor, C.N. Gilmore, Pat Philo, P.O.R. Smiley, Harold Wilshaw, Bryan A. Reid, Michael Jackson, Richard Parkes, David Lacelles, Bernard O'Brien, Christian Tyler, Rodger Milton, D.I. Lewty, Mrs Colin McFadyean, Tony Garnett, J.M. Throp, Mick Coplen, Roderick Acton, Nick Garland, Dennis Jawet, K.D. Moran, B.S. Reed, A.J. Cradwell, D.S. Rowbottom, Andy Vince, W.H. Bauld, Robert Young, Maxime Molyneux, T. Langley, Natalie Carrol, Caroline Platts-Mills, David Monro, Kathy Freeman, Andrew Kay, Rebecca Sinclair, F.E. Petty, Tessa Fantoni, John Naughton, P.T.L. Kohler, N.J. Pearce, R. Frensham, B. Quigley, N.B. Holmes, J.N. Behrens, R. Coulthurst, Jan Karpinsky, Brian Locke, Peter Mullins, the editors and staff of *Private Eye*. Those whose names I have overlooked are asked to forgive my primitive filing system.

The source material appeared in the following:

News of the World, Yorkshire Gazette, North London Press, Daily Telegraph, Daily Express, The Times, Time, Paris-Presse, Reading Standard, Guardian, London Property News Letter, Evening News, Bizarre (Paris), Dauphiné Libré, Der Kurier (Vienna), New York Herald Tribune (Paris), Daily Mail, Sunday Express, Kayham (Persia), Sunday Mail, La Réalité Depasse La Fiction, Sunday Times, Daily Herald, Morgenpost (Berlin), Slough Observer, New York Times, Courier de Paisuboeuf, Yorkshire Post, Combat, Lancashire Evening Post, Wiltshire Times & News, The Australian, Rolling Stone, Daily Mirror, Scottish Daily Express, Irish Times, Stoke Evening Sentinel, Evening Standard, Hull Daily Mail, Daily Sketch, Llanelli Star, Honolulu Advertiser, Sunday Telegraph, Glasgow Herald, Harlaw Citizen, Borneo Bulletin, Brazil Herald, The Sun, Sunday Mirror, Kenya Sunday Nation, Surrey Herald, Morning Star, Worker's Press, Oldham Evening Chronicle, The People, Rochester Democrat and Chronicle, Birmingham Evening Mail, Newcastle Evening Chronicle, South London Press, Sunday Nation, Calgary Herald, Ottawa Journal, Bradford Telegraph, Washington Evening Star, Southern Evening Echo, Los Angeles Times, Westmorland Gazette, Scotsman, World Medicine, The Railway Magazine, Philadelphia Bulletin, Disc and Music Echo, Cape Argus, Der Spiegel, Southern Evening Echo, Istanbul Daily News, Bangkok Post, Irish Times, Times of Gambia, Roswell Daily Record, Newsweek.

The Publisher wishes to thank the owners of the drawings by Mr. Kitchen reproduced herein.

Many of the stories originally appeared in the Four Square edition of True Stories (1965), all the stories appeared in *Private Eye* at one time or another.

CHRISTOPHER LOGUE

"After I found my first wife in bed with the milkman, my second with the postman, and my third with the chimney-sweep, I came to the conclusion that the source of the trouble lay with my bed. There was something wrong with it," said Mr Johann Huber during his trial for arson in Munich. "As I dislike acting hastily I decided to have another go before getting rid of it – so I married Martha. She was a perfect wife. She made me forget everything. The trouble was her mother.

"On the first night she slept in the bed with Martha. I had to use the divan. Next morning she presented me with a set of rules saying when I could and could not make love. It was too much. I was only allowed in the bed once a month. The rest of the time her mother, and at the week-ends her mother's friends, slept in it."

After a year of this Mr Huber decided to burn the bed. Unhappily the fire spread to the neighbouring houses and some £42,000 worth of damage resulted. He was given two years.

As part of a national campaign for greater public safety, the Japanese Government subsidised experiments into the nature of landslides.

During the first of these, a total of 15 people were killed and the viewing public saw an entire television unit swallowed up by the cliff whose motions they were photographing.

Shortly before his marriage, Mr John Adams of Stoke-on-Trent allowed a guest to fix a massive ball and chain to his ankle. When the time came for him to approach the altar the key could not be found.

Thus married he humped the ball to the reception and hid it under the table while he made his speech and drank numerous toasts.

He was released by the fire brigade in time to start his honeymoon.

During the Late Windsor period the practice of money-lending in Britain was given a spectacular boost. The tax-payers were encouraged to buy articles priced beyond their current resources provided that they agreed to pay, within a given time, a substantially greater sum than the price they could not originally afford.

Among the debtors was a Scot named Gavin Clyde. Gavin, like the rest of us, wanted a better car; and, like the rest of us, want was his master.

Outside the garage of Mr Arthur Smith, a Glasgow car-dealer, Gavin observed the vehicle of his choice – a Fiat 600. He examined it, approved it, and, in return for a small van plus £150, possessed it.

Later in the year Gavin realised that whenever he drove his Fiat a large black car followed him. Tiring of this he stopped and asked his follower what was going on.

The follower identified himself as an agent of The Friendly Finance Company. He claimed that Gavin was driving a car that did not belong to him. As proof of this he produced Agreement DF/IBG/91274053/70.

Gavin told himself that the law was on his side. He had paid for the Fiat. The Fiat was his.

In this he made a mistake. The law was not on his side. The law sides with those who act legally.

It was useless to say that the man who sold Gavin the car was the Company's true debtor. The Company was created to feed its shareholders; its feet were firmly on the ground; except where its own interest was concerned, truth was irrelevant.

At first Gavin's solicitor advised him to keep the car, but when the Company increased their pressure the solicitor changed his tune and advised its return.

This Gavin did. He was poorer by one van, £150, and his solicitor's fees. He had also been cheated by Mr Frederick Smith, the brother of a man outside whose garage the car had been offered for sale. Naturally Mr Arthur Smith was mystified: if his brother chose to sell a car on which there were outstanding payments, and if that car was parked outside his garage . . . well, that was not his concern.

Gavin felt defeated. At least the matter was closed. Now he could save and buy a new car.

These plans were disturbed by the arrival of a Sheriff's Officer at Gavin's house. This official told Gavin that The Friendly Finance Company were suing him for the depreciation of the car, plus interest on the depreciation, plus the expenses incurred in repossessing the car.

Unless he paid up within seven days, the Sheriff's Officer said, they would take the furniture out of his house and sell it to meet the debt.

Gavin did not have enough money to meet the debt. His solicitor advised him to declare himself bankrupt, thereby using the law to frustrate the law.

Gavin complied – forgetting that bankruptcy is a serious matter.

The GPO removed his phone; unreliable people are not allowed telephones. He could not continue in business; bankrupts are forbidden to make business. He could not continue to buy his house; sequestered men may not use building societies. He could not emigrate; Dominions bar debtors.

In addition he had to pay twenty guineas to declare himself bankrupt.

You may wonder what happened to Mr Frederick Smith.

Nothing.

"Of course," a leading solicitor explained, "Gavin could sue. But I don't advise it. It would be extremely expensive. Even if he won his case – and there's no guarantee he would – Mr Frederick Smith could say he was bankrupt. And then where would he be?"

An abundantly leafed twelve foot high growth rewarded Mr Fred Kreckler for the care he spent on his favourite garden plant.

Photographed with his darling, Mr Kreckler's picture appeared in the local newspaper.

The next day he was arrested.

The plant, *Cannabis Sativa*, had grown from accidentally scattered birdseed.

As part of its "Make London Fun" scheme, the Greater London Council have organised a visit to the New Cross Sewage Farm at Abbey Wood: "We think of it as an alternative attraction to the Henley Regatta and the Crystal Palace Pop Fest," a spokesman said, "possibly for older people."

Visitors to the farm will be shown over a 2,500 ton sludge dredger, a fully electric tip barge that deposits the former's cargo far out at sea, an operational 19th century beam engine, and they will be able to try on the latest equipment for rescuing workers who have fallen into the vats.

"We think it will prove a great attraction," the spokesman continued, "Abbey Wood is among the largest effluent stations in the western world. Every day we deal with over 115 million tons of organic waste from South London alone."

After making love to his friend's wife, Mr Johann Heer of Vienna took a felt-tipped pen and drew a romantic landscape on her bum.

"I am a regular Sunday painter", said Mr Heer, "and after we had enjoyed ourselves, Frau Garubul wanted to watch *Gone With The Wind* on television.

"Love stories do not interest me", he continued, "so I took up my pen. I did not ask her permission. Later I went to sleep. She was gone when I woke up".

Returning home, Frau Gambul got into bed just before her husband, Franz,

finished his stint as a late-night taximan.

"As my wife was asleep when I got in, I thought I would give her a goodnight kiss. It was then I saw the landscape – signed with Johann's name. It was his signature," Franz went on, "and to prove it, I woke my wife up and we compared it to another signature on a painting he gave us that hangs in the dining-room."

He was granted a divorce.

Mrs Winifred Skilbeck liked to exercise her dog beside the River Ouse. One morning while they were enjoying their walk Mrs Skilbeck noticed something in the river. As it was some distance away Mrs Skilbeck could not be sure what it was.

However, Mrs Skilbeck's curiosity had been roused. After a few steps she sat down and waited to see what it was. She put it down as a water-hen.

In ten minutes her patience was rewarded. Mrs Skilbeck saw that it was not a water-hen. It was an old man.

"He had grey hair and he was facing me," she said, adding, "I was puzzled because he had his jacket on."

"He was ashen-faced and coughing," Mrs Skilbeck said.

Mrs Skilbeck waited until the old man had drifted out of sight before she turned to go home. A man was walking along the bank. He, too, was exercising his dog.

Mrs Skilbeck stopped the man and they discussed dogs for a few minutes. Just before they took leave of each other Mrs Skilbeck said:

"As you're going downstream see if you can spot an old man floating about. One went past just now. I was puzzled because he had his jacket on."

The man said he would. "It's strange for someone to be in the Ouse with his jacket on," he added.

When Mrs Skilbeck and her dog reached home she said to her husband:

"Is it usual for a man to be in the river with his jacket on?"

Mr Skilbeck did not think he was usual.

"I don't think he should have been in the river in that state," Mrs Skilbeck said.

"Perhaps he was a frogman," said her husband.

"I don't think he could have been a frogman," she said, "he wasn't wearing a helmet."

Mr Skilbeck said that there had been some frogmen about.

"Not ashen-faced frogmen," said his wife.

Some hours later Policewoman Flaherty called on Mrs Skilbeck. Policewoman Flaherty said that a woman called Mrs Bielby had been exercising her dog beside the Ouse when she saw an old man in the river.

Mrs Skilbeck was able to confirm Mrs Bielby's story.

Policewoman Flaherty thanked her and left.

The coroner's verdict on the man was death by drowning.

After buying two hundred tropical birds, Mr William Foyle, a slaughterman, of Basildon, built them an aviary.

On the day it was finished he got a letter from Basildon Urban Council ordering him to demolish the building because planning permission had not been granted.

Mr Foyle went out and bought a lion.

"I keep her in the yard," he said, "the Council will have to deal with her if they want the aviary down."

"We have nothing against Mr Foyle's lion," said a spokesman for the Council. "Planning permission is not required for a lion's den, but aviaries are a different matter."

The Council have refused Mr Foyle permission to build a horseshoe-shaped ranch in which to breed lions.

"I am appealing to the Queen," he said.

In addition to these problems Mr Foyle is homeless. He burned down the £5,000 farmhouse in which he was living.

"It was an eyesore," he said.

At the completion of her act, Miss Diane Woodward, a stripper, is dressed in no more than a G-string. Thus arrayed she was assaulted by an eight foot boa constrictor on the stage of a London club.

Seeing Miss Woodward's danger her fellow strippers rushed onto the stage and unwound the snake. The usually silent audience received this variation on a conventional theme with acclaim.

Wynfryn Jones was seventeen when he met Elsie Saunders. They fell in love, and, to celebrate their engagement, bought a motor-car. He contributed £100 she contributed £50.

In the days that followed Mrs Saunders pictured herself at the wheel as she drove her child (recently fathered by Jones) to a grand reunion with her three other children, fathered by Mr Saunders – who had divorced her.

Only Mrs Saunder's inability to drive prevented the excursion. She mentioned this to the milkman and, on his recommendation, visited an instructor called Wilson. Wildon's coaching was excellent. In no time he and Mrs Saunders were good friends.

Young Jones was not suspicious; even when Wilson moved into their house as a lodger he did not complain. But when he came down one morning and found that the log-book of the car bought by Mrs Saunders and himself to commemorate their engagement was made out in the name of Wilson and not the name Jones, he felt the time had come to act.

Confronted with the log-book Mrs Saunders explained that her plans had changed. She was going to marry Wilson instead of him.

"I changed the name in the log-book because we'll need the car on our honeymoon," she said.

Mrs Saunders wanted to avoid any unpleasantness. Jones would be welcome in the house as a lodger.

"It's up to you," she said, adding that she and Wilson were not sleeping together.

Jones left.

"One night when we were in bed together," said Wilson, "the dressing-table started to move. Jones emerged from behind it and assaulted me with a coat-hanger."

As Mrs Saunders opened the window to attract a passer-by Jones produced a dinner knife. Wilson leapt from the bed to defend himself.

Counsel asked Jones: "Is this the knife?"

"Yes."

"Wilson came at you naked and defenceless?"

"Yes."

After a few minutes Jones went downstairs.

"Who's coming down to get it first?" he shouted.

Nobody answered.

Jones remounted the stairs and asked for the scarf he had left behind the dressing table.

Wilson and Mrs Saunders leant against the door.

When Jones had gone home Mrs Saunders went downstairs and found her vacuum cleaner was in the garden and her dinner knives stuck through the letter-box.

Later the police charged Jones with assault and burglary.

On the 28th of March, 1958, police were called to a caravan situated in a field outside Lakeview, Ontario.

The caravan contained two men and was spattered with eggs. One of the men was dead. His face was covered with shaving cream and he held an egg in one hand.

The other man, who was unconscious, was dressed as a jockey, had a sheet round his shoulders, a salad bowl on his head, and coat-hangers draped over each ear.

"We are holding the jockey for questioning," said the police.

At an exhibition of public library books misused by citizens by citizens the centre-piece was a copy of Shakespeare's collected works with "FISH AND CHIPS IN THE OVEN – MAKE SOME FRESH TEA" written across the title page.

While out for a day's angling, Mr Keith Smith, an Australian jockey, was drowned when the fish he hooked pulled him into the Murray River.

While Mr Albert Cooke was walking his dog outside his home in Walsall, Birmingham, a car drew up beside him out of which stepped a man dressed in the uniform of the RSPCA.

The man was carrying a gun.

Without more ado he approached Mr Cooke and shot his dog. He then charged Mr Cooke seven shillings and sixpence for the removal of the dog's body and drove away.

The police are investigating.

Everyone had settled in for the late night showing of *"And Woman Was Created"* in the Classic Cinema, Llanelli, when the manageress, Mrs Melita Royle noticed some "troublemakers throwing cigarettes about the cheaper seats." Quick as a flash Mrs Royle unleashed Sabre, her tame police dog. "Sabre soon had them out of their seats, down the stairs and into the gutter," she said. "All the serious cineasts applauded.

"Decent people need have no fear of Sabre," she continued, "he is as tame as a mouse until he is commanded to rout the trouble-maker. I discovered his efficiency when a police handler demonstrated how he would attack under command. The handler put out his hand towards me and Sabre had the sleeve off his jacket in ten seconds flat. While I was managing the Classic in Chester he took off a trouble-maker's trousers during *'Ben Hur'*."

On December, 1962, the trial of Karl Mekis, Chief Commissioner of Public Security for The Republic of Earth, was held in Weiner Neustadt, Austria.

This Republic is part of The Solar Commonwealth, a mutually beneficial system of satellites ruled from Venus, the "home" planet. The President of The Republic of Earth is Franz Weber-Richter. He was not in court but in Rome, waiting the return of his Security Chief, and hoping for substantial additions to The Republic's treasury.

President Weber-Richter's first contact with the Venusian Pan Planetary Commonwealth was in 1942. At that time, he (who in addition to his Presidency claims to be the illegitimate son of Adolph Hitler) was enjoying a tour of occupied France with his dad.

During the tour the Venusians landed near Fontainbleau, interviewed the Fuhrer, appointed him First President of The Republic of Earth, and returned home until worldly hostilities ended. Unfortunately, when this day came the Fuhrer was not in a position to take his place in the Venusian Cabinet. They asked Weber-Richter to help them out. He agreed – and was taken to Venus for a period of indoctrination.

At the time when the Fuhrer and his son were becoming acquainted with the Venusians, Karl Mekis was serving on the Eastern Front as a member of the SS police. By a stroke of good fortune Karl Mekis abused SS discipline, and was severely punished. When the Allies triumphed, he was released from prison, shown every courtesy, and employed as an informer for the CIA. Herr Mekis was not content with this modest role. In next to no time his ambition led him to be a key figure in the Austrian black-market. He was caught and dismissed.

Soon after his dismissal he boarded a tramp steamer bound for Chile. The only other passenger on this vessel was President Weber-Richter, who lost no time in exposing his identity to Herr Mekis. In much the same vein Herr Mekis told the President that he was the victim of a Jewish black-market conspiracy. These mutual confidences formed the basis of an endearing friendship. By the time the boat reached Chile, Weber-Richter had given Herr Mekis an important post in his first government.

Mixing and carrying meal for Weber-Richter's chickens was not an exalted portfolio; however it kept Herr Mekis occupied while his President toured South America raising funds.

Weber-Richter raised fifteen million pesos. The money came from Nazi refugees who form substantial minorities in several South American states, and who, from their past experiences, were well supplied with cash and credulity.

The money bought a large house in Santiago, moved Herr Mekis off the chicken farm, and translated him to the rank of chief butler to the President.

There followed a period of intense activity; an office and three secretaries were engaged, a bodyguard of peasants recruited, a stream of edicts, decrees, laws, economic plans, and a Constitution of 629 pages (setting out the powers of The First Venusian Republic on Earth) were printed and mailed to German speaking people all over the world. They invited the recipients to place themselves under the protection of the Republic before the revolution (scheduled as "X-Day") began; all the documents maintained that X-Day was imminent.

Money poured in – much of it from Europe. One man, Herr Fretschner, a respectable publican, contributed DM 20,-000 and expressed his wish to visit Chile and to prostrate himself before the President.

The time came when the contributors, especially those living in Santiago, got restive. The President called a meeting at his house, prepared an elaborate statement, and booked two seats for himself and Chief Security Commissioner Mekis on a plane to Rome.

The two cabinet ministers faced their supporters with confidence. Everything had been well spent, the President told his assembly; some of it on staff, some on printing, some (but only a fraction) on personal expenses; the major item on the Republic's books was the cost of telephone calls to Venus.

That evening the cabinet ministers left for Rome. They rented a villa outside the city, the President married the foster-child of an Italian Princess (she became Minister of Culture) and the Chief Commissioner of Security was dispatched to Vienna to collect the European deposits.

As he stepped off the plane he was arrested.

"Waiting for X-Day has been a great strain on all of us," Herr Mekis explained to the court. "You must not think we wasted the money. Certainly not. Why, the new suit I had ordered in which to meet the Venusian Admiral when the 5th Space Fleet landed had to be cancelled to pay our milk bills."

"It makes me very angry when people say there are no Venusians. Everyone cheers when the Americans send a rocket past Venus, but when I suggest the Venusians can send a rocket past Earth I am put in prison."

"The President will think I have betrayed him. He is waiting for me."

President Weber-Richter will have to wait for five years; that is to say, the period during which his rival Republic (Austria) has ordered their Prison Commissioners to detain his Security Chief.

Apologists for South African racism will be delighted by the appointment of Mr James Moiloa to the academic staff of Bloemfontein's University for Whites, known to local humourists as the "Free State" university.

He will not, however, be known as a "lecturer" but as a "pronunciation aide;" this example of verbal dexterity being occasioned by the Minister of education's refusal to allow black Africans to "lecture" only "aide".

Professor Kok (sic), the Free's liberal Rector said: "This decision makes history – we fought and we won a long battle over Moiloa."

Not wishing to alarm the voters the Rector went on: "As all the students learn Bantu from language laboratory tape recorders, Moiloa's function is that of a machine."

The Japanese version of General Motors is called Toyota Ltd. Its President is Mr Shotaro, an octogenarian, who – at a cost of £168,000 – has erected a shrine to commemorate the souls of those killed by and in Toyota cars.

This road memorial covers 600 square feet and is made of blood red concrete. It is sited among the pines of Tateshina, an exclusive mountain resort, where senior executives of Toyota Ltd often build summer homes.

Mr Lewis Sutter, a 71-year-old company director states that he has played more than 150,000 games of solitaire during the last ten years.

He has compiled the results of each game in six massive ledgers. "I play about 40 games a day," he said. "Solitaire doesn't interest me all that much. But I can't think of anything else to do."

During a service for dumb animals Prebendary May was obliged to descend the steps of the sanctuary in St Paul's Church, Covent Garden, and to eject a member of The Performing Animals Defence League.

The congregation was composed of dogs, monkeys, cats, Alfred, (Prebendary May's mynah-bird who sang in a loud, clear voice), and a golden retriever owned by Mr Marcus Latouche.

When the Prebendary asked Mr Latouche's retriever: "How many Apostles had Our Lord?" a man from the League leapt to his feet and complained that the question was cruel.

After the man's ejection Prebendary May repeated the question. The dog barked twelve times.

Eric Mason, a bee-keeper, a student of the Bible, and the father of fourteen children has been given five years in prison.

Some time ago Eric married a young woman called Lorna and took her to his bee farm on the Murray River some two hundred miles from Melbourne.

In the fullness of time she bore him seven children and, in order to give her some help with the housework, Eric invited another girl called Jean Guy to live with them. Everything went well. The two women got on together.

Three years later when Eric moved his hives from one forest of flowering gum-trees to another, there were four extra children to move with them. These children were Jean's and Eric was their father.

Apart from the fact that Lorna had her marriage lines and Jean did not, the family was very happy. To prevent any quarrelling Eric decided he would marry them both. The ceremony went off smoothly; Lorna signed the register as witness.

But eleven children are quite a handful, and to ease the labour another young lady, an English immigrant called Ruth, joined the household. In next to no time Eric impregnated her; nevertheless Ruth did not complain about anything, saving her lack of marriage lines.

To equalise her status Eric hit on the following plan. Jean, disguised as a man would take Ruth to the nearest registry office and marry her. They cut Jean's hair short, dressed her in Eric's clothes, and, with Eric and Lorna as their witnesses, the two were wed.

Time went by and Ruth added three children to the ménage.

So they lived in reasonable contentment, keeping their bees and producing their children. But all good things come to an end. Some neighbours complained; Eric was arrested and imprisoned.

The only result of this action was that the women were separated, the children left fatherless and ashamed, and the family broken up.

"Eric was always a marvellous husband," said Lorna.

Soon after the wedding of Mr Stanislaus Lembke to his bride Katharina had begun, the guests noticed that the groom looked miserable. When the priest came to that part of the service in which the couple are reminded of their future marital responsibilities, Stanislaus rushed out of the church and threw himself into the river Danube.

"I can't understand what came over him," said Katharina.

Above an audience of 5,000, and under the big top of Oklahoma City, the trapeze artists Don Martinez and Lucy Fanfan were married by Bishop Ezra Nero of the Landmark Spiritual Temple.

Bishop Nero, suspended 75 feet in the air, shouted out the vows to Mr Martinez and Miss Fanfan as they arched to and fro.

Disaster overtook both finalists in this year's Mark Twain Memorial Frog-Jumping Tournament, held in the writer's home at Hartford, Connecticut.

Fierce preliminary contests left two Iowa frogs, "Beadle" of Sioux City and "Big Dick" of Oskaloosa, deadlocked with matching 87-inch three jump totals

In order to get a clear decision the rule forbidding physical encouragement by owners was waived.

"Beadle", spurred by a slap on the jumping table, managed 66 inches in two jumps, but died of a heart attack on landing; while "Big Dick", after his owner fired a starting pistol, leapt off the table into the mouth of "Sunny", a guard dog used for patrolling the literary shrine at night.

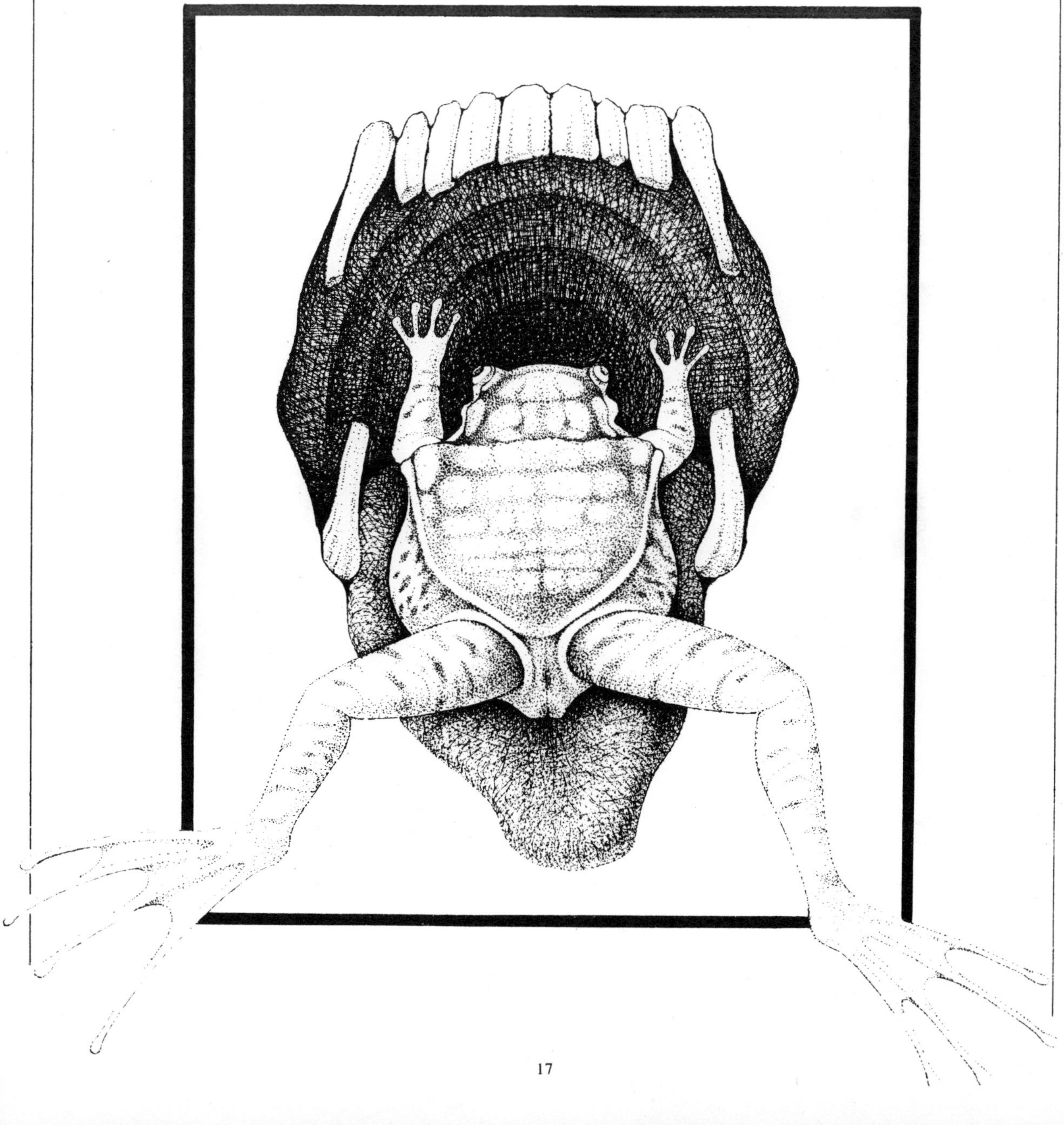

Well armed riot police dressed in bullet-proof jackets were called to the scene of the first serious accident involving two pedestrians.

Mr Soeren Van Nielsen, aged 79, and Mr Holger Lund, aged 82, entered a pedestrian crossing from opposite ends in Town Hall Square, Copenhagen. Both men had their heads down and were in a hurry.

Passers-by heard a sharp crack and saw the men fall to the ground.

Captain Haag of the Special Police said: "The victims are now in hospital suffering from concussion. We are not sure if the crack was made by their skulls meeting or from a faulty exhaust pipe."

After he had killed one of their fellow tribesman in a car accident, Mr Peter Howard, an English planter living in New Guinea, was informed by the Jiga that he would have to pay them £465 and four head of cattle. When he refused to do this the dead man's family gave him a good thrashing.

Next day he handed over the money and the cattle; then, as compensation for the thrashing, the tribe presented him with £10 and a pig.

A ball, driven from the 10th tee of Quinindo golf-course by Mr Robert Wilson, struck a tree, penetrated the windscreen of a passing moped, and lodged in the driver's mouth.

For twenty-five of his fifty years Fred Sherborne earned his living as a street sweeper. Tom, his brother, was a man of different stamp: a lifetime spent in local building earned him wealth and civic respect. He was a member of Bideford Town Council.

In late middle age Fred decided it would be nice to own a house, and, as this desire coincided with an attack of pneumonia, he used the visit paid for by his brother Tom to bring the subject up.

Tom said he had a nice little cottage in Bideford that would suit Fred and his wife perfectly. It was a snip at £270.

Although Fred did not have this sum to hand, his unblemished record as a minor public servant, plus his brother's standing as a local businessman, persuaded The North Devon Building Society to lend Fred the money against a mortgage on the cottage. The deal went through. Brother Tom was paid £270.

There was only one snag: the cottage was occupied by an old age pensioner.

"The tenant was eighty when I sold Fred the cottage," said Councillor Tom, "it was reasonable to assume he'd get possession in three years at the most."

The optimism inspiring this hope was frustrated. The old age pensioner survived twelve more winters.

"Tom said we could get him out," said Fred, "but my wife and me didn't want to evict an old man."

Fred paid for his weakness. The cottage fell into ruin before his eyes and every time he tried to repair it the pensioner created dreadful scenes.

"Meantime we rented another house from Tom," Fred continued, "it wasn't in good shape at all – only thanks to having a good cat we kept the rats down."

Eventually the pensioner died and Fred moved in.

The first letter he received in his new home was from the Council. It informed him that the cottage was to be demolished because it was an eyesore.

"What could I do?" said Councillor Tom. "The best thing Fred can do is to take the matter to court."

Fred ignored his brother's advice. He asked a local demolition expert how much it would cost to destroy his cottage and found he could not afford the figure quoted. The Council, however, insisted that the job be done.

And so, during his fortnight's annual holiday, Fred hired a sledge-hammer and demolished his home himself. When the work was finished the Council cleared the site, sold the rubbish, and charged Fred £24 for the job.

Fred wrote and explained he could not meet their bill. The Council answered that they were unable to grant him time to pay; instead, they suggested he sell them the site and made a preliminary offer of £30.

"The trouble is," said Fred, "I still have to pay a ten year mortgage off, and my wages only amount to eight pounds a week."

A few days later the Council wrote to Fred saying that unless he paid their bill they would claim the site.

A small-ad:

Madame Basile, teacher at Saint-Quentin, requests the people who read her correspondence before she receives it not to keep the letters for more than 24 hours.

A swan, driven from its native haunt by inclement weather, landed on the sidecar of a motorcycle being driven through the centre of Bath.

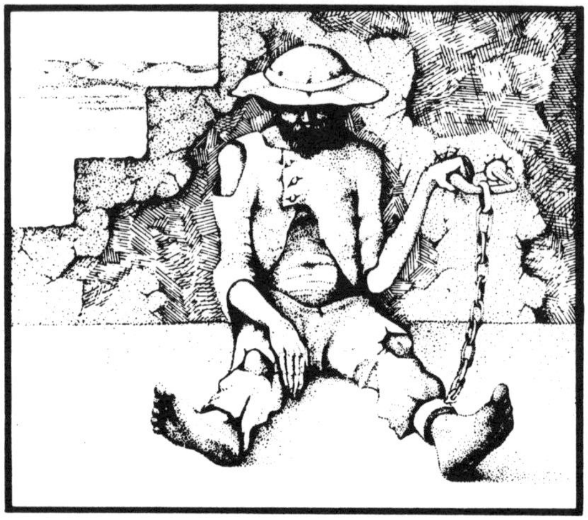

Mr and Mrs Clavenna of North Italy have been imprisoned for keeping their eighty-year-old uncle chained to the garden steps for a year.

Explaining his action, Mr Clavenna said: "We did it for his own good. His eyesight is very poor and he might have eaten some of our fruit from the orchard."

Mrs Lula Scroggins of Honolulu was picking greens for her Sunday dinner when an acquaintance, Mr Newton Foster, peered through the greenery and said: "I am going to bite Shoo Shoo Baby."

Shoo Shoo is Mrs Scroggins dog.

"I went down to the doghouse and sure enough there was Newton down on his knees with his teeth sunk into Shoo Shoo's neck."

After his arrest, Mr Foster said"I have nothing against dogs. I just felt like biting one – so I did."

When Cicero Gonzales, a poor peasant of Pernambuco, saw a train steaming towards a length of line he knew to be flooded, he ripped off his wife's skirt, and waved it madly, and averted a disaster in which – the Railway spokesman said – hundreds of lives might have been lost.

Invited to receive his reward, Gonzales discovered that he had signed a contract to work for the Line for eight years at £3 5s per month.

"We cannot understand his complaints," said the spokesman. "It is our privilege to create work opportunities."

Ruth Buckley, the right half-back in a ladies' football team was offered a lift home by Richard Whittington-Asquith, a 27-year-old gentleman of independent means.

On the way home Whittington-Asquith made a strong pass at Miss Buckley. She asked him to stop and said that she was a virgin. Mr Whittington-Asquith replied that love-making would improve her football.

Miss Buckley continued to refuse his advances so Whittington-Asquith blacked her eye.

The judge gave him nine months and his trial was watched by his ex-wife, 71-year-old Mrs Whittington-Asquith, from whom he was divorced last year.

Finding that her husband liked sleeping with their baby's dummy in his mouth, an American wife asked him if he would like a bottle made up to go with it. He would, so she did, and thus they continued for several years. Eventually the wife became anxious; not, she assured the journalist to whom she wrote for advice, because either of them felt unhappy, but because her husband is a senior executive on the Apollo Programme.

Doctor Alvin Singer of The American Electronics Laboratory has invented a pessary into the rim of which is built a small transistor radio. When the ovulation period begins the female's temperature rises and the radio starts to broadcast a signal. This signal is picked up by an antenna placed near the bed, warning the lovers to disengage or resort to other means.

Over a period of 45 years Mr Ernest Colville of East London worked for the firm of Thomas Ward as a sorter of scrap metal.

At the close of his retirement ceremony, and after pocketing his £17 whip-round, sixty-five year old Mr Colville stepped towards the works manager who handed him a cigarette, lit it and wished him good luck.

"I was astounded," said Mr Colville.

"Colville is making a fuss over nothing," said the firm's spokesman.

Twenty hours after he crucified himself as a sacrifice to world peace, Professor Patrick Tamao, a Yoga scholar from Santo Domingo, came down from the cross on medical advice.

Arrested for assault after hijacking a policeman at knifepoint by jumping on his back and ordering him "To walk to Cuba", an unnamed New Yorker was characterised by his arresting officer as "some kind of a nut. He fainted when I told him it meant three refuelling stops."

Shortly after visiting her dentist, a housewife of Daytona Beach, Florida was awakened in the middle of the night by her husband who complained that her teeth were broadcasting. He was right.

Her dentist, Dr. John Long, explained that certain metallic fillings when contacted by acidulous saliva can create a receiving set.

"It will pass off in a few days," he said. "Meantime keep your mouth closed as much as you can, for its natural cavity forms an effective baffle box, thereby increasing the volume."

The lady did as she was told and the broadcasts ceased. "I thought I was free of the trouble and ready to throw a party," she said. "But no sooner were things under way than I opened my mouth to laugh and out came the theme song from *Doctor Zhivago* followed by *Rambling Rose*. Fortunately our friends are all broadminded. Some of them even danced to the tunes."

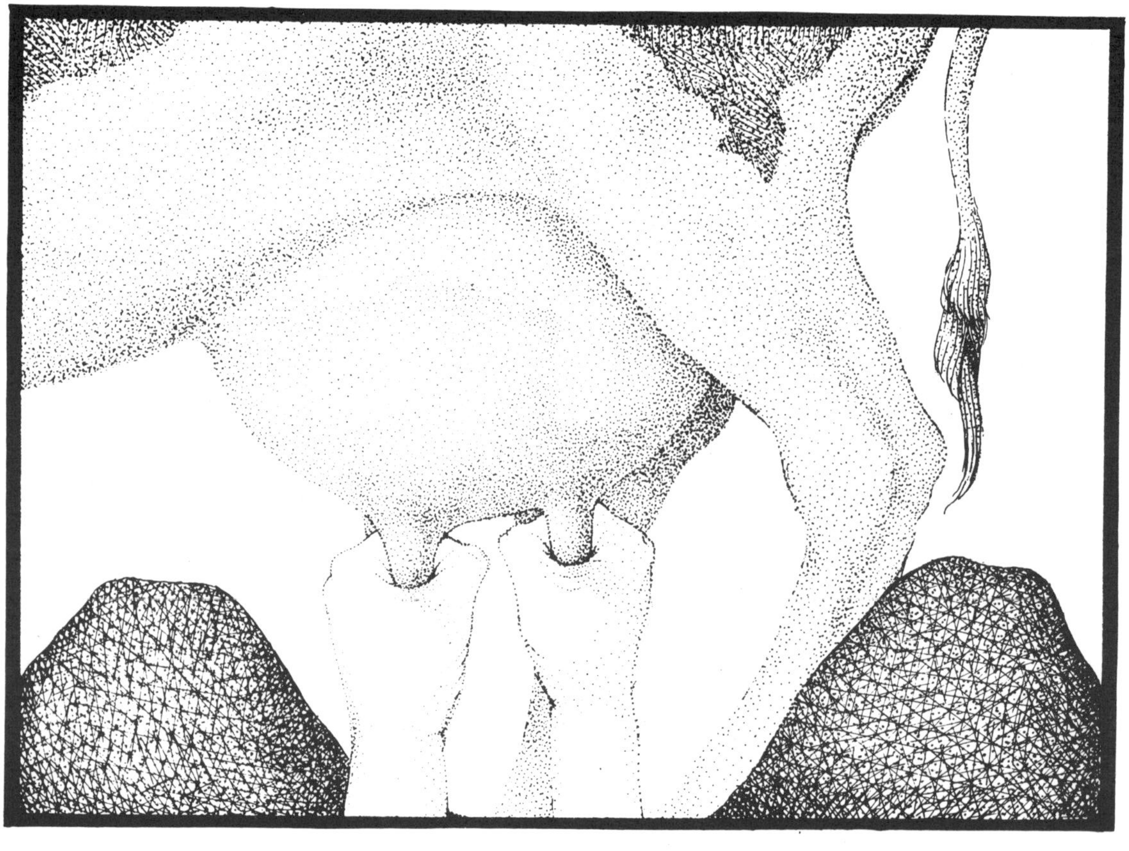

Mr John Pearce, the captain of Notts, Lincs and Derbyshire Rugby Union Fifteen has been obliged to withdraw from their match against Warwickshire because a cow sat on his knee and broke his ankle.

Mr Pearce was milking the cow on his Bakewell farm when the accident occurred. "My cold hands must have caused it," he said.

Devoted to the promotion of religious sentiment among the landed and those who work their land, the Cheshire Baptists Association mounted a theological sideshow at the Royal Lancastrian Agricultural Fair.

Observant Baptists, recognising the decline in national piety, realised that after four hours standing about in the wet peering at sullen livestock something exciting would be needed to kindle awareness of guilt among even the most primitive citizens.

After discussing they agreed to show their potential converts a tableau representing An Ideal Bible Family, composed of a stern but honest father, sitting beside his obedient, kindly wife, with their innocent daughter poised between them; all three would be crouched over the good book, at whose open pages the hand of a fourth figure, depicting a wise Baptist minister, would point. Such an icon, they felt, could not fail to disarm the skeptical and hearten the shy.

Reverend Allcock was put in charge of the production.

Lacking serviceable dummies for his tableau, Reverend Allcock appealed to Madame Tussauds of Blackpool for aid, and when (and promptly) Tussauds replied how delighted they would be to abet so devout a scheme, he was overjoyed. But this simple emotion changed to delight as, having disposed his dummies and opened the show, Reverend Allcock watched the landed and the landless neglect their differences and flock to see the tableaux.

It was some time before he realised that other than religious motives inspired their attention.

The dummy representing the wise minister was none other than that of Doctor Crippen; the honest father turned out to be the likeness of a notorious swindler; the obedient wife was composed of the Queen's body topped by the head of a famous ice-skater; and the innocent daughter was Snow White – who, as we all know, lived in the woods with seven midgets.

The town of Debreczen in north-west Hungary was the home of a man called Janos Dey.

Dey was married to a nagging wife. As he did not want to get rid of her he spent a good deal of his time considering how she could be brought to her senses. Finally he evolved a plan in which fear and guilt would play important roles.

He would fake suicide.

Dey constructed a safety harness and climbed into it while his wife was doing her shopping. Shortly before she was due back he got into the harness and suspended himself, a convincing corpse, from the ceiling of their bedroom.

His wife returned, and seeing what she believed to be her dead husband, she screamed and fainted.

The woman living next door heard the scream. She hurried over to see what had happened.

She found what she thought were two corpses.

Not one to miss an opportunity the woman decided to loot the flat before she fetched the police.

As she was slipping out of the bedroom with various items under her arm, the hanging corpse lifted its foot and gave her a good kick.

So great was the shock she died of a heart attack.

Dey was acquitted on a charge of manslaughter. He told the court that his wife's nagging had stopped.

An elephant was washed ashore in Widemouth Bay, Cornwall. The police believe it was thrown overboard from a passing ship.

Mr Ongesa Ngo'Nga, a seventy-seven-year-old ex-postman from Nakuru, Kenya, was arrested while carrying two ten foot high sisal bags.

On examination the bags were found to contain 135 lb. of dried *Cannabis Sativa Africanensis* from the Kisumu district – a crop reckoned by many to be the finest grown on the Dark Continent.

When asked what the sacks contained, Mr. Ngo'Nga said: "The sacks are full of sweetener. I am taking them to the city for my uncle, Mogusu Ngo'Nga because his car is out of order."

Smokers will appreciate that 135 lb. equals 2,100 oz, equals 21,600 new sterling pounds (ex-London Airport).

Mr Ngo'Nga was fined £45.

Alarmed at the number of young people sent by their parents to borrow Ian Fleming's adventure stories, Mr Peter Henderson, a Northumbrian library worker, said:

"This must stop. Children under 14 will not be issued Mr Fleming's books, or other books with *risqué* chapters.

"What happens once the book is in the family home is a parental matter. But youngsters could easily be disturbed if they opened such a book on the road. I feel I am responsible while the the book is *en route*.

"Adventure stories are ideal reading for adults," Mr Henderson continued, "but they will have to call personally.

"Besides, I want more adults to call and see our full range."

Mr Henderson is 23.

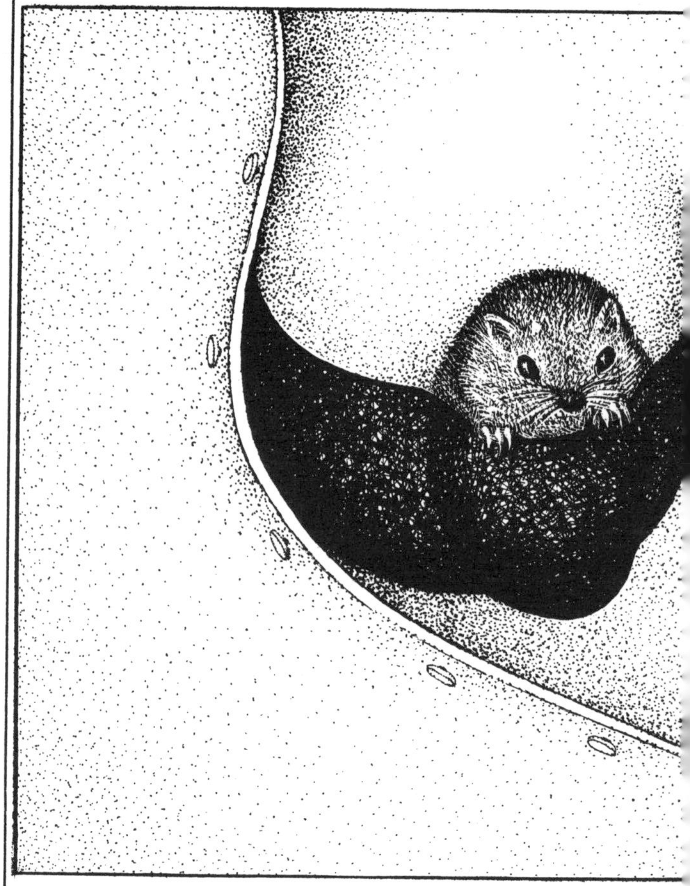

While answering a charge of indecent ass had been bitten by the young lady's brassere.

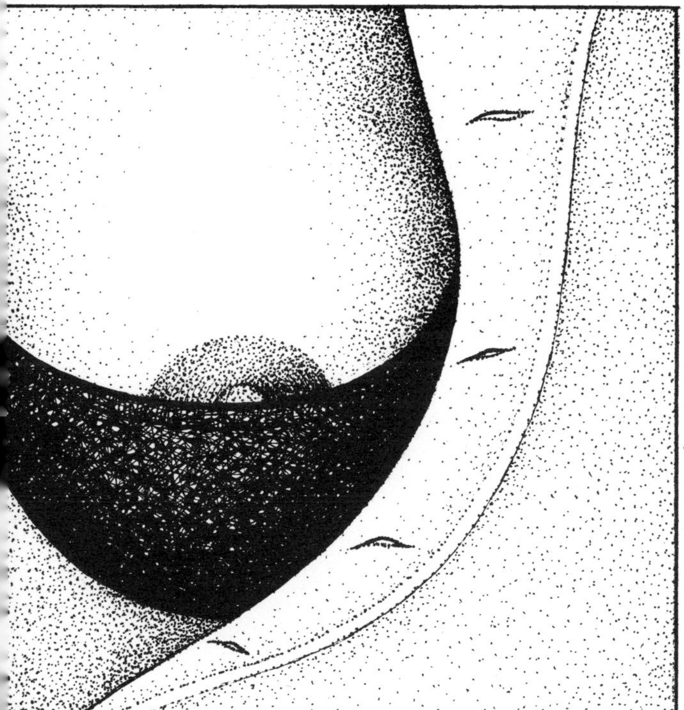

he defendant revealed that he
uinea pig which lived in her

On a fine evening towards the end of May the Edinburgh police were informed that a breach of the peace was taking place in Holyrood Park, a large, open place that was once a garden but is now covered with ashphalt and used for military parades.

When the constables arrived they found James Gaithen, a man of no fixed abode, hopping about in the roadway and trying to retrieve his wooden leg which he had removed and thrown at the passing traffic.

The constables warned him that he was disturbing the peace. Gaithen, however, just shouted abuse at them and threw his leg at another vehicle.

Introducing a motion regretting the Mayor of Hounslow's decision to abandon the traditional mayoral robes during his term in office, Alderman Denton said:

"These elements of colour add dignity to the chamber."

"I'm an avowed traditionalist myself", said Councillor Crispin, "When Alderman Pauling strode into the council chamber with his robes floating behind him, it was the glory of Hounslow."

Alderman Alf King said that it was the mayor's free and democratic right to wear whatever he wanted; as far as he, Alf King, was concerned, Mayor Slattery could wear a wetsuit in the chamber.

At the end of the meeting the 24 Conservatives rose in deference to the mace. The 47 Labour councillors remained seated.

Before a congregation of some 120, the Reverend Clifford Lacey of St. John's, Eltham, began the nuptials of Rosemary Nicholson and David Mullett – a former choirboy.

The words "Dearly Beloved . . ." had scarcely passed the Reverend Lacey's lips when the bride's brother nipped out from behind the pulpit and panned across the faithful with his cine-camera, finishing the shot with a close-up of the verger, George Tubby, aged 72, a veteran of two world wars.

Reverend Lacey told Mr Nicholson to clear off; Mr Nicholson refused; whereupon, to the amazement of the devout, a shouting match developed between them, to which Mr Harry Nicholson, the bride's father, soon added his voice.

The Reverend Lacey said that he had not given permission to photograph the choirgirls.

Leading schoolgirl Anne Butterbub said: "I feel sorry for the happy couple."

"Get on with it", said the bride's father, "he's not using lights."

Towards the end of the ceremony, a bagpiper dressed in a kilt walked down the aisle playing *Amazing Grace*. This disturbed the organist, Mr Beam, who played the theme from *Dr Zhivago* (the bride's personal request) all the louder.

Later, in the vestry, there was, according to the Vicar, "some jostling".

The bride's father, a retired paratrooper, said: "If the Queen can have her wedding on film, so can Rosemary" – and challenged the Reverend Lacey to a fight. Several wedding guests began to dance among the graves, and, when Mr Tubby thrust his offertory plate towards them, it was knocked into the air.

"The bagpiper is a relative," shouted Mr Nicholson. "This do cost me a tenner, and I've thrown it away."

Mr Tubby said: "I've done a couple of hundred of these in the last few months, but this one beats the lot. I was abused by the majority of the guests, and all I got for the job was 50p."

Mr Nicholson, the bride's father, has written a letter of complaint to the Archbishop of Canterbury.

During a case brought by the citizens of West Covina, California, against Mr James Davis, in which they alleged that his pet chimpanzee, Moe, was a dangerous beast, Judge Crumb said: "From what I've seen of Moe it is better behaved than a lot of humans that get brought in here."

Moe was dressed in a check shirt, yellow whipcord trousers and two-tone bootees. When acquitted he jumped onto the bench and shook Judge Crumb by the hand.

When Mrs Alva Mays of Muleshoe, Texas, heard that her sister-in-law had been injured in a freeway pile-up, she set off by car to see her.

Entering the Santa Monica Freeway at 9.18 am, she began a journey of nearly 1,000 freeway miles that included 16 unsuccessful negotiations of the downtown Los Angeles interchange, a night in Bakersville, six traffic violations for both fast and slow driving, 12 hours trapped in dense fog on the Oceanside overpass, and an extensive survey of nine separate freeway systems from which she emerged three days later by driving through the barrier protecting the new four mile extension of the Garden Grove Freeway, where she crashed into the crowd attending the opening ceremony.

Although separated from the Zoo snack bar by a moat, Chicago's seven polar bears had shown considerable interest in the building for over a year.

When the keepers arrived after a night of heavy rain they found the moat flooded and the bears gathered around the bar, all seven smothered with the marshmallows and icecream they were busily eating.

In 1958, in Buenos Aires, there was held The Gran Primo de la Republica Argentina – a race involving some of the fastest drivers and the most dangerous vehicles then in existence.

Although the start was not until late afternoon the stands had been packed since midday and late-comers, finding their seats occupied by enthusiasts with tickets identical to their own, obliged the early arrivals to defend their foresight with vigour.

Five minutes before the start the drivers (Fangio, Hawthorn, Ascari, Farina, and Gonzales) were shocked to find their cars surrounded by fighting spectators who spat, struck, cursed, and kicked each other in full view of the excited throng.

One disappointed ticket holder produced a pair of wire-clippers and snipped his way through the fences guarding the circuit.

President Peron arrived. The Chief of Police told him what was happening. The President raised his hands and replied:

"Let my children go!"

Encouraged by this the spectators flowed across the circuit as the flag went down and the drivers accelerated through the happy crowd killing three people.

Conditions beside the distant parts of the circuit were similar. The poor, unable to afford either genuine or forged tickets, were standing in thousands by the tricky hairpins; many of them were tired from waiting and leant against the road signs, obscuring them; but when the drivers appeared their energies were restored. Taking off their coats they ran across the bonnets of the cars, shouting: "Toro! Toro!"

On the 21st lap Farina's car caught fire. Swerving to avoid a child who ran across his line he got into a high speed slide and slammed broadside into the crowd, killing about 15 people. Their sacrifice was wasted. The boy Farina tried to miss was slain by a following car.

Farina was carried off in a state of collapse and two ambulances arrived. Overcome with excitement their drivers turned straight into the circuit and set off the wrong way round, "to show the crowd a bit of real speed," they said later.

One ambulance driver lost control, rammed the grandstand, loaded it up with those he had injured, and continued as before.

Although the professional drivers had retired, the race was far from over. The police ignored their President's orders and tried to clear the circuit by using stock-whips on the crowd. One policeman paid highly for his zeal; he was dragged off his horse and kicked to death.

The only vehicles left on the circuit were the ambulances whose drivers refused to go to the hospital, and a number of family cars whose owners were determined to keep the show moving. President Peron made a brief, personal appeal for order before he left to open a new school. The Police, utterly defeated, sat in the grandstand, and, as the drivers left for their hotels the entire circuit was covered with outraged spectators belabouring each other because the race had been cancelled.

The Queen's Muffin Maker, Mr Daniel Tong, has had seven ducks and fourteen chickens killed by a fox.

Mr Clarence Ramsay was standing on the pavement outside his home in Houston, Texas, when a man came up and stabbed him in the back. Turning round to face his assailant Mr Ramsay was surprised to hear him say: "Sorry – I thought you were somebody else."

Mr Bejoy Khar came from Pakistan to Birmingham.

Each week he put aside a little of his earnings. He was saving for a summer suit.

"I even kept myself short of food," he said.

Eventually he had the right amount – £30; he collected his suit and put it carefully away.

In May Mr Khar went south for his annual holiday. The following day he took his suit out of its cellophane wrapping and walked in its elegance beside the river Wye.

He had covered no more than a hundred yards when he saw a small dog struggling for its life in the river. Mr Khar leapt in to save it.

"Not till I was in mid-air did I remember my suit," he said.

He landed on a bank of deep black slime.

The dog, annoyed at having its swim disturbed, gave Mr Khar a nasty bite and swam ashore wagging its tail.

"The funny thing is, I don't really like dogs," said Mr Khar.

To find their champion, two hundred National Ambulance Servicemen sat beside and fished into a stretch of canal near Kidderminster. After five hours competitive angling a passer-by told them that all the fish in the canal had been moved to another water three weeks ago.

A new contest has been arranged.

While taking refreshment in the Half Moon Hotel, Herne Hill, Mr Alec Graham became involved in a discussion whose final stages obliged him to place a head-lock on his fellow disputant.

"It wasn't a serious fight," said Mr Hyland, Landlord of the Half Moon and former middleweight boxing champion. "Alec put the lock on this chap who reached up and tore off his ear. I picked it up, handed it to Alec and told him to get it sewn back on, but he just laughed and threw it back on the floor.

"When we closed I took the ear round to Alec's house. He just took it out of my hand and threw it in the dustbin. I was amazed."

Some time later, the police called at the house, retrieved the ear, and took it, plus its owner, to hospital where it was stitched into position.

"All I have to say is that we've shaken hands and made it up." said Alec.

Mr Djambi and Mr Hasnuddin of Haruku, Indonesia, both laid claims to the same sago tree. As property lovers and strong traditionalists they decided to settle the matter in the time honoured way – by seeing who could remain underwater the longest.

Watched by their fellow villagers the rivals weighted themselves with stones and jumped into the sea.

Both drowned.

Complaints laid by the Reverend Donald Pattison of Chelmsford have obliged that town's Art Festival Committee to withdraw a painting from their current exhibition.

The painting showed Christ playing poker with friends.

"I am quite sure Christ did not play cards," said the Reverend Pattison, "and certainly not after rising from the dead."

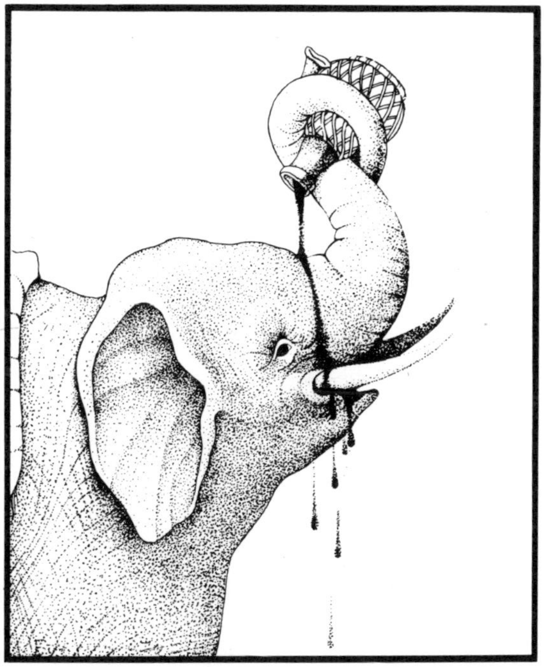

Deciding to go to a wedding by elephant, four citizens of Islampur – a town in Uttar Pradesh – began their celebrations while still mounted. Now and again they let the elephant have a swig – until it blundered into a power line, killing itself and its riders.

Having shot at and stabbed two intruders, Mr Ernest Underwood, a retired hairpin manufacturer of Los Angeles, ripped off their stocking masks to discover his 52-year-old daughter and his estranged 71-year-old wife.

The police said: "It was a family matter."

After an intensive but fruitless search for a negative precedent, the police of Ecorse, Michigan, have issued a gun permit to a blind man.

Two years ago seventy eight year old Mrs Elizabeth McClelland left Belfast, Ulster, and went to Christchurch, New Zealand, in order to avoid street violence.

Last week she died in a Christchurch hospital after being hit over the head with an Irish civil rights placard during a demonstration.

Having pleaded guilty to the charge of murdering her lover, Orlando, Miss Ertha Lee Griffin was given 10 years probation on condition that she pays the court £7 per month for the next four years, obtains a high school diploma in Civics, and goes to church every Sunday.

Judge Ed Claudeward said: "I am not a regular attender myself."

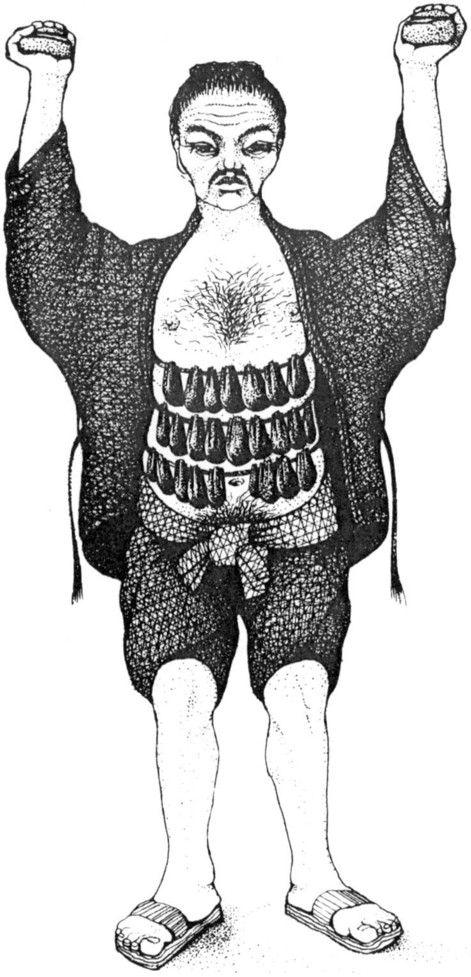

Arrested for the theft of two cream buns, Mr Shoichi Fujita of Kobe was found to have 3,000,000 Yen taped to his stomach.

"I have been saving for years," he said, "and I found that the best way to do it was not to spend."

Students attending Chichester College of Further Education have been advised to sing *God Save the Queen* while frying bacon.

Mrs Ivy Davey, their instructress, said: "*God Save the Queen* has a running time of about two minutes – just right for each side of a rasher."

Mr Vincent Lally, a salesman from Up Holland, explained that he was exceeding the speed limit because the hot black puddings he was about to deliver had steamed up his speedometer.

Earlier in the year the Cooperative Wholesale Society placed an order for 10,000 pairs of three-legged trousers with a firm of industrial tailors.

"Once we join Europe", a Co-operative spokesman said, "competition will intensify. It is essential for Britain to maintain her lead. Three-legged trousers are something completely new. They will make a fantastic dent."

After suffering cuts and bruises and being carried unconscious from the wreck of a Thames Valley bus in which she had been travelling, Mrs Florence Parrott received two shillings worth of postage stamps from the company by way of compensation. The accompanying letter explained that 7d had been deducted from the fare she paid; this sum represented the two stops passed before the accident.

Professor Mohammed Bikhtami's claim that his theft of 295 tables, 340 typewriters, 959 roll-top desks, 1,069 chairs, and 27,056 paper clips, was an academic exercise, seems to have been accepted by the governors of Isfahan University, Iran.

On being released from prison, he was made Professor of Criminology at the same university.

A convention of eunuchs has been called at the Sukkur, 315 miles north of Karachi, to decide on their policy for the next general election in Pakistan. A spokesman for the eunuchs said: "We are typical conservative voters. We see no need for change."

Among a troup of entertainers visiting Parramatta Goal, near Sydney (Australia), was 23-year-old Sharon Hamilton, a singer of uplifting folk melodies.

Hardly had she finished the opening stanza of "We shall Overcome", when Leonard Lawson, a rapist, leapt onto the stand and, holding a knife to Miss Hamilton's throat, asked the audience to leave the room as he wanted to be alone with her.

Two of his fellow prisoners overpowered him. Miss Hamilton had five stitches in her throat.

Several hours after finishing a three-year sentence Mr Britton Batley was re-arrested for being in possession of 5 cwt of copper roofing belonging to the prison authorities.

The truck, which had met him at the prison gates and into which the copper had been loaded as he was released, was stopped by the police at Prestwich.

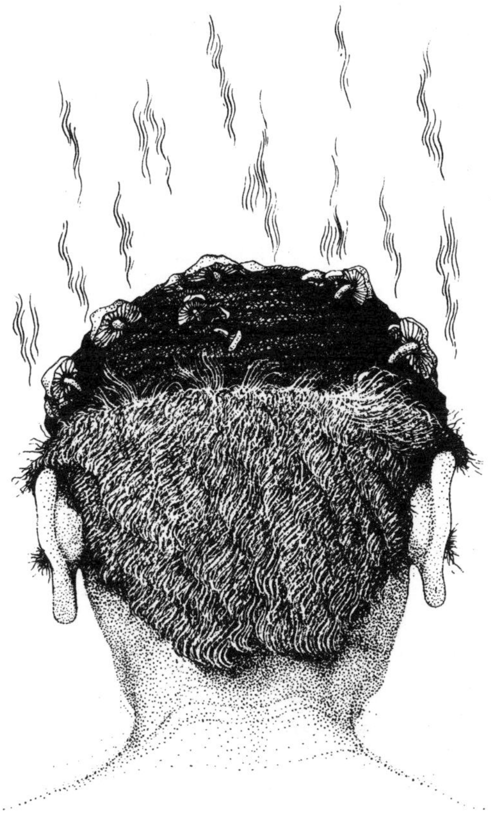

"Twelve years ago I went bald; now I have a two inch growth of silver curls," said Mr Harry Biggs of Peterborough. Mr Biggs, who is 70, attributes the revival to his interest in market gardening.

"For some time I have been in the habit of rubbing my hands over my head after repotting my plants in mushroom manure. There is a mushroom factory in my back garden," he went on, "and six months ago I started this new mulch. I have not rubbed on anything else. My hair is now two inches long and still growing."

A farm labourer from a village in West Flanders made love to his daughter of fourteen and was sent to prison for three years.

He served his time with patience, but when the day of his release drew near he became anxious and full of shame. He thought his wife would never forgive him; he did not dare show his face at home; he asked the Governor if he could be kept in prison for ever.

The Governor was worried, too. He had been informed that, while the labourer was serving his sentence, his wife had been sleeping with a neighbour; now she was pregnant.

On the day of his release the labourer told the Governor his fears. "You had better keep me locked up for ever," he said.

"Anyone can do what is wrong," the Governor replied.

"No," said the labourer, "not anyone. Only bad people."

"Suppose your wife had made a mistake?" the Governor said.

"Oh, Sir, I would be the happiest man alive. We would be evens."

"Well," said the Governor, "I have to tell you that your wife has given birth to a child, and that the father is a neighbour of yours."

The labourer began to laugh and to cry, he kissed the Governor, he jumped up and down with joy.

When he reached home he told his wife that she was forgiven, that he is forgiven, and that from now on she must not see the neighbour.

The same evening he invited the neighbour to supper. The three of them drank and sang together and the labourer said:

"Go upstairs, do everything you want, as much as you can, for the last time."

This they did.

Since then the neighbour has stayed away, the labourer and his wife are happy, and the baby is well cared for.

Arrested for having a cosh in his car. Mr Warren Stewart of Streatham, explained that it was not a cosh but a small rubber hammer known in the motor repair trade as a "windscreen-clouter".

The windscreen-clouter was in his car and not on his work because he intended to chop a piece off it to repair his wife's oven.

He was fined £15.

Having lit the fire in the grate of his cottage near Didcot, Mr Derek Langborn, a specialist in the molecular theory of anti-matter, popped outside to fill his coal scuttle.

When he returned he noticed that the fire had spread from the grate, and that his log was burning merrily away.

Mr Langborn took the log-box in his hands with the intention of carrying it into the garden; however, on his way out he brushed against the front door curtain. By the time he returned both the curtain and the door were afire.

At this point he decided to call the Didcot Fire Brigade. Unfortunately, before he could dial their number, he observed that the log-box, (which he had placed at a safe distance from the cottage), had ignited his motor-car.

Wrapping himself in his overcoat, Mr Langborne made his way to the car with a pail of water, tripped over a partly filled petrol jerrycan, and, to his amazement, watched both his vehicle and his Mermaid roses illuminate the night.

By this time, alerted by his neighbour, (the local Rodent Officer), the Didcot Firemen were on the scene. They, after helping Mr Langborn out of his smouldering overcoat, doused the several blazes. "I am going to switch to electricity," he said.

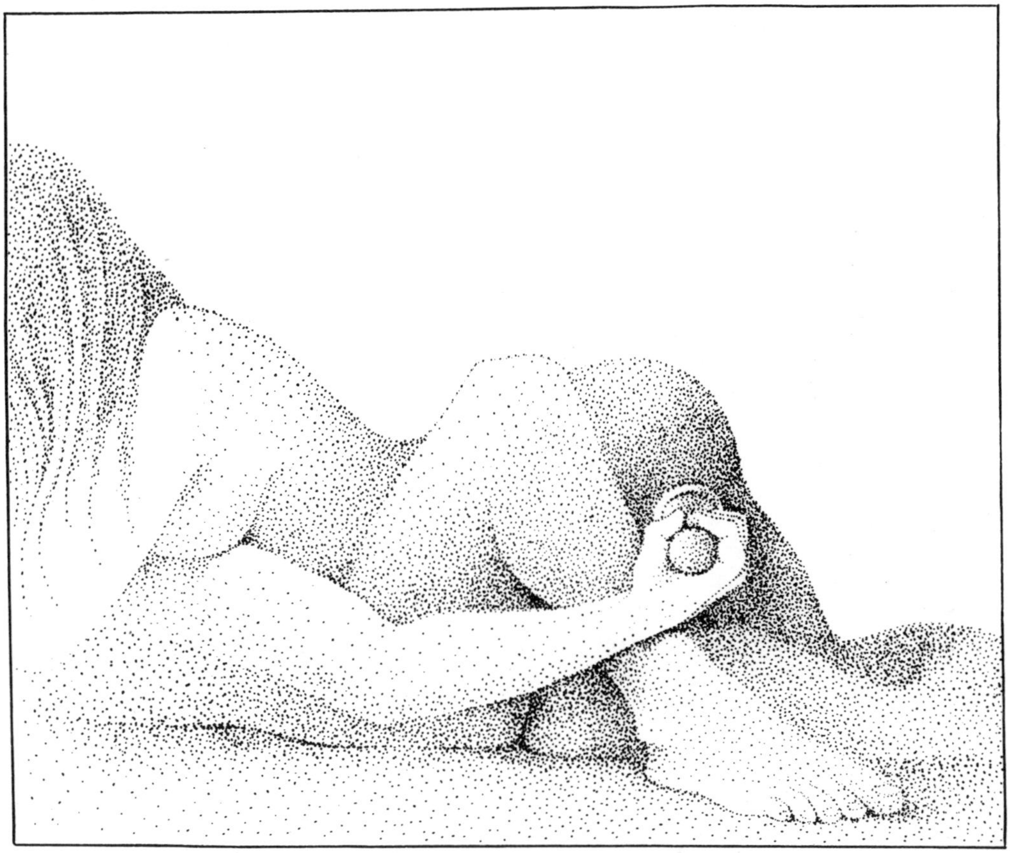

On the day before her divorce Mrs Ursula Becker of Dortmund called at her husband's office to discuss the settlement of their property. In the course of her visit Mr Becker argued against their action, but in vain. However, when the judge asked her to tell the court how long it had been since they made love, Mrs Becker was surprised to hear her husband shout: "It's a lie!" when she said: "At least 18 months ago."

"We made love on the floor of my office yesterday morning!" said Mr Becker. "I marked her arse with the office date-stamp."

Mrs Becker's petition was denied.

At three in the morning a policeman observed a party formed of two men, a woman, and a large alsatian dog, walking down a London street. One of the men carried a ladder, a camera, and a torch.

After a whispered conversation the policeman allowed the party to proceed.

They stopped outside a house, waited until the people living on the ground floor finished some interior decorating, then placed the ladder against the sill of a first floor window.

When the man reached the window he flung it open, leapt inside and cried: "He is here!" Then, turning his torch on the couple in the bed he took a photograph of them – convincing evidence, he hoped of his wife's adultery.

The presiding judge asked if he could see the photograph.

"I was so excited I forgot to take off the lens-cap," answered the man.

The wife explained that the man with whom she was in bed had had all his teeth out that day and she had just made him a bowl of soup.

Granting the divorce the judge said: "I think the dog was a red-herring."

A barge enthusiast, Mr John Tait of Oxford, was steering his vessel down the Kinksey Canal when he encountered a bridge too low for it to pass.

Observing 64 ramblers coming along the tow path, Mr Tait invited them aboard as ballast.

Unknown to Mr Tait, the barge was holed just above the waterline. Even as it began to sail under the bridge, so it began to sink. Without more ado, the 64 ramblers hopped back onto the tow path. The barge responded, rose, and jammed itself between the surface of the water and the underside of the bridge.

"I see only one possible solution," said Mr Tait. "We shall have to lower the water level of the canal."

Mr Bob Bush, a Los Angeles City spokesman, explained why the city Council has planted 2,000 rubber trees down the middle of its main street.

"They are there as a monument to The Synthetic Society," he said. "We already have an extruded all Chippendale and Adam council chamber, polystyrene golf-grass verges, non-milk coffee whitener, and weather proof high forgivability tombstones, so why not go the whole way?

"And at 50 miles an hour what motorist will see any difference? Anyway, our maintenance costs will actually make us a profit over the next thirty years. You give the tree-ettes a bi-annual dusting and an annual rinse; transplanting, pruning, bed-weeding, leaf-collection, and artificial manures are all unnecessary. What's more, we have a 75 year non-fade guarantee on each plant. That is rationalisation at its best."

Mr Victor Nusenbaum of Gosforth, Newcastle, was driving his three-week old Elan motor car along Grandstand Road when he heard a loud noise from the back of his vehicle.

No sooner had he stopped than the car burst into flame, and, before the fire brigade arrived, it had melted and poured away down a nearby drain. All that remained was the engine and the headlamps.

"It is a terrible thing," he said, "to see your new sports car draining away."

The *Wiltshire Times & News* is not a famous newspaper. A few weeks ago the staff made a modest bid for immortality: they printed a "pen-portrait" of a local worthy by the name of Harris.

Within hours of publishing, Mr Harris had asked the *Wiltshire Times & News* to make the following corrections:

After leaving the Far East, Mr Harris served for four years in Ireland, and not, as stated, six months.

Mr Harris did not, as stated, farm for three years at Heddington. He farmed at Coate Lodge. He did not farm, as stated, at Coate Road.

Mr Harris has never, as stated, taken a special interest in bicycling and walking.

Mr Harris did not, as stated, have an eye removed at Chippenham Hospital.

Mr Harris was not, as stated, involved in an air-raid on Calne.

And Mr Harris is not a member of 54 hunts.

During the trial of Mrs Agnes Neep of Dunfermline, Sheriff John Mowat heard witness testify that she had subjected her children, Edward, aged 8, and Elizabeth, aged 7, to the following:

Thrown the boy over her head down a concrete path; struck him so that his leg was broken; hit him with a bottle because he could not tie his shoelaces; forced him to smoke a cigar: beat him with a dog-leash; put him in a bath of ice-cold water: the girl had been put in a dark coal cellar.

Finding the case of ill treatment against Mrs Neep "not proven", Sheriff Mowat said that though being held by the hair and ankles over a bath of cold water at 11 p.m. was not a comfortable experience for the boy, "it was not an act likely to cause him unnecessary suffering, and while the coal cellar incident might have been a frightening experience for Elizabeth, it did not amount to cruelty because the cellar door had not been locked."

Postmaster Bradbury of Leeds had just finished smoothing the cement of his forecourt when Chip, a local dog, trotted across it.

Mr Bradbury warned Chip off, resmoothed his cement, and was easing his back when Chip did it again.

Mr Bradbury hurled his shovel at Chip, following it up with a kick. The kick landed on Mr Rowley, Chip's owner.

Mrs Bradbury, who had observed the incident, decided to call the police. A similar decision was taken by Mrs Rowley.

Mrs Bradbury reached the telephone first. She had dialled the first of the three nines when Mrs Rowley pulled her out of the box by the hair.

While settling their differences both ladies fell into the cement.

It was at this point that Mr Bradbury's mother-in-law, Mrs Stevens, decided to intervene. Both she and Mr Bradbury were pulled into the cement by the infuriated wives.

Mrs Stevens is in her late eighties.

Outraged at the behaviour of his neighbours towards his wife, Mr Rowley charged across the road and carried Mr Bradbury and himself back into the cement.

All five voters then waded into the cement and each other.

The magistrate, Mr Walter Smart, said: "You'd better forget the whole thing."

While on trial for theft Mrs Farida Halim gave birth to a seven pound boy in the dock. Without hesitation she named him Bara – "not guilty" in Arabic. The case was adjourned.

During an action for divorce the judge asked the wife for an example of her husband's behaviour. She replied: "Last year Harry asked me if I had anything to discuss before the football season began."

The Californian Supreme Court have been asked to remove Judge Leland Geiler from the bench because he is in the habit of using a battery-operated dildo as a gavel.

After sentencing a man to 1,500 years for rape the judge said that it struck him as a reasonable punishment. "500 years would have been just a slap on the wrist."

As a man convinced that seeing is believing, New York Judge Irwin Nebron transferred his court to The Bottoms Up night-club before pronouncing its current floor show decent or otherwise.

Both Judge and jury watched Mr Joseph Ferreri and Miss Setters perform a Dance of Love whose climax seemed to represent copulation on a bearskin.

Unable to make up their minds about the dance the jury asked to see it again – after which they enjoyed an encore given by under-studies.

Detective George Ulrich understood the jury's reluctance to pronounce: "It's a difficult matter," he said. "The police have watched the show 75 times."

Asked by a lady if he had felt sexually aroused, Detective Ulrich said: "I don't think police officers are responsive to normal stimuli."

The case has been adjourned.

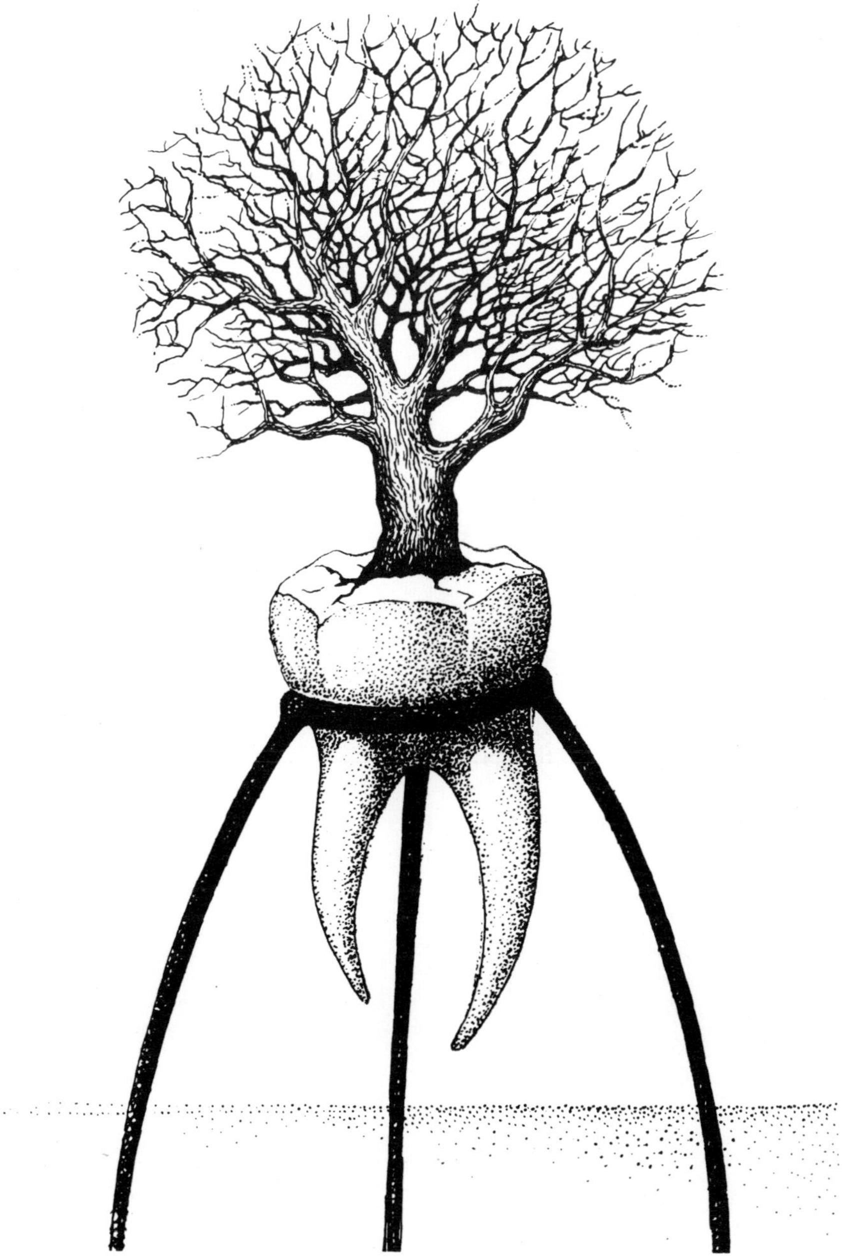

Mr James Scott, a fashionable dentist and bonsai fancier, has succeeded in growing a miniature oak tree in a hollow tooth.

During a judicial enquiry at Bangkok, Colonel Chalaw Uthockpatch, head of Thailand's Special Branch, said that the ghost of the Thai Superstar, Milly Challibanquer, had appeared at his home and asked if its photograph could be taken.

Miss Challinbanquer's death, which was caused by her fall from a helicopter, had been an occasion for Thai national mourning.

"My wife and I were resting," he said, "when we felt a chilly sensation and our hair stood on end. I concentrated hard and saw Milly's ghost clinging to a sundial in the garden.

"When it asked me if it was possible for a ghost to have its portrait taken, I said yes, but it would have to contact the right photographer and muster all its powers; only then would it condense sufficiently for a 400 ASA film with electro-flash to get a crisp image."

Asked if he could see Miss Challibanquer's spirit clearly, the Colonel said: "Not as clearly as in former days. She has not quite recovered from the multiple injuries resulting from her fall. I told her that it might be as well to wait for a few months until she was herself again."

The enquiry was occasioned by the arrest of certain left-wing trouble makers who had denounced the apparition as a fraud designed to cover up the illegal importation of camera equipment.

The Colonel concluded: "My department silenced these atheists. It is a well known fact that ghosts can appear in photographs. My wife has snaps of President Lincoln and President Roosevelt, both of them taken after death."

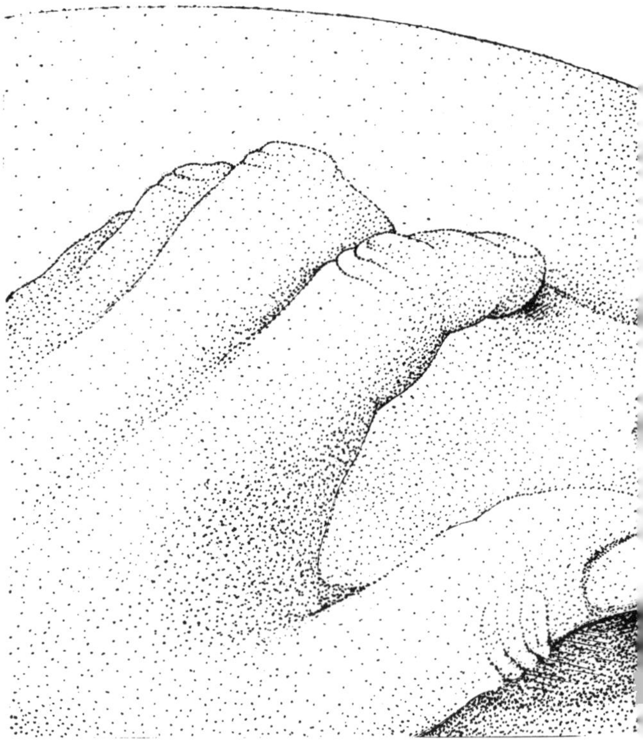

The Journal of the American Library
publication of *Playboy* Magazine in a B

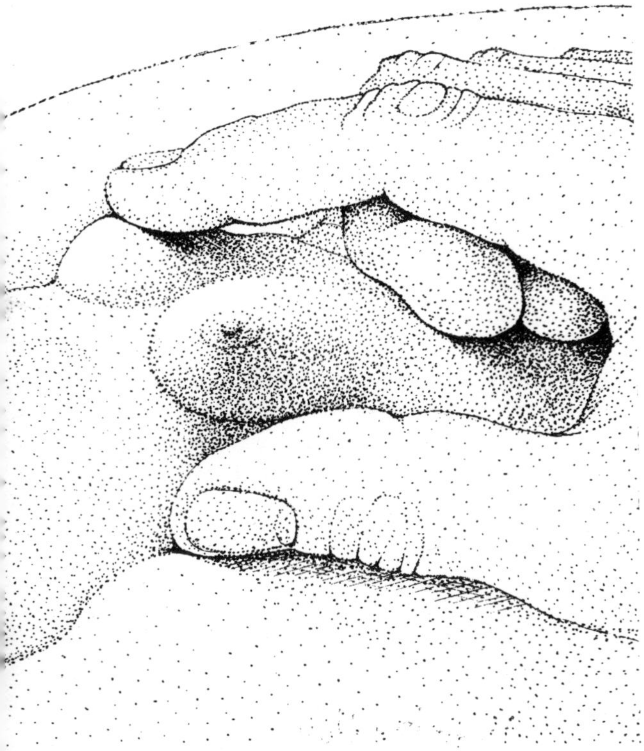

sociation has announced the
: edition.

Miss Jennifer Walton was an art student. Usually she lived in London but sometimes she occupied premises in Hampshire.

John Carter, a married man of thirty-five, came to the door of these premises, knocked, and when Miss Walton went to see who was there he explained that he was not feeling very well.

Miss Walton invited him in and brought a glass of water.

While drinking the water Carter told Miss Walton that he was suffering from painter's colic. He finished the glass, lay down on the floor and asked Miss Walton to stand on his stomach.

"The best cure is a weight on the stomach," he said. Miss Walton stood on his stomach for a minute.

"He told me I wasn't heavy enough," she said. "I fetched a box but that wasn't heavy enough either."

Feeling that she had done everything in her power to help Carter, Miss Walton suggested that the large man who lived next door might bring express relief.

"A large woman would be preferable," said Carter.

"I fetched Mrs. Stone from next door," Miss Walton continued, "and we stood on his stomach together."

After this Carter felt better.

The Magistrate bound him over for twelve months.

Over-excited by the opportunities for free enterprise a young Pakistani sold the same house 86 times for a total of £29,000.

After scoring with his left foor, right-wing Aly Mahmoud Elefesh of Elmasanea collapsed from excitement. He kept shouting "Goal! . . . Goal! . . ." until he fell unconscious, was transferred to a nearby hospital and died a few moments later.

Mr Miguel Garrido, an upholsterer of Bobigny, France, has been awarded damages because he can no longer hold tacks in his mouth after an accident whilst playing blow football.

A monkey has succeeded in thumbing a lift from Nice to Cannes.

In spite of the three explosions that occurred in a car park directly opposite the hall where he was speaking, Mr David Bleakley, the late Minister of Community Relations in Northern Ireland, said: "I have never been prouder to be a citizen of Belfast than at this time. Protestant and Catholic, rich and poor, are maintaining a standard of community stability that compares with anything that has ever been recorded in the annals of Europe". Mr Bleakley was addressing the annual meeting of the Ulster Instititute for the Deaf.

Eleven years ago, two black citizens of Florida were sentenced to death for rape. This year they will be taken from prison for re-trial.

Judge Charles Scott implied that their chances of acquittal were quite good as the lady in question can no longer remember whether she was raped or not.

Sixteen months after the first of its bi-weekly issues, an American newspaper whose editorial policy was to print no news save good news has closed down.

Called *Good News*, published from Sacramento, and with a circulation in all 50 of the United States, the paper did not announce its own failure.

"Such an item would have been against our policy," said its founder, Mr William Bailey – father of twelve. "But we learned a lot of interesting facts, the most important being that the public really want good news, good news, good news all the way. Certainly I lost $200,000 – what does that prove? Nothing. It is the advertisers that are to blame. A paper full of happy-fun-yummee laughs puts people off buying fancy compensation durables, so we got no advertising. As soon as I have another two hundred thousand I intend to start all over again."

The last issue of *Good News* contained the following headlines: "196,459,483 citizens were not killed in auto accidents this year". "Fantastic drop in suicide rate". "No war declared in sixteen weeks". "Triple rapist enters monastery".

While admiring his roses, Mr Frank Mole, a 73-year-old citizen of Ludgershall, was amazed to see a fox head across his garden and into his sitting room. This feeling escalated when a pack of 20 hounds followed the fox and tore it to shreds in front of the fireplace.

Mr Milutin Veljkovic, an electrician from Belgrade, has broken the world record for staying underground. Accompanied by a pair of Canadian ducks he has remained below for 463 days. During this period his wife has divorced him.

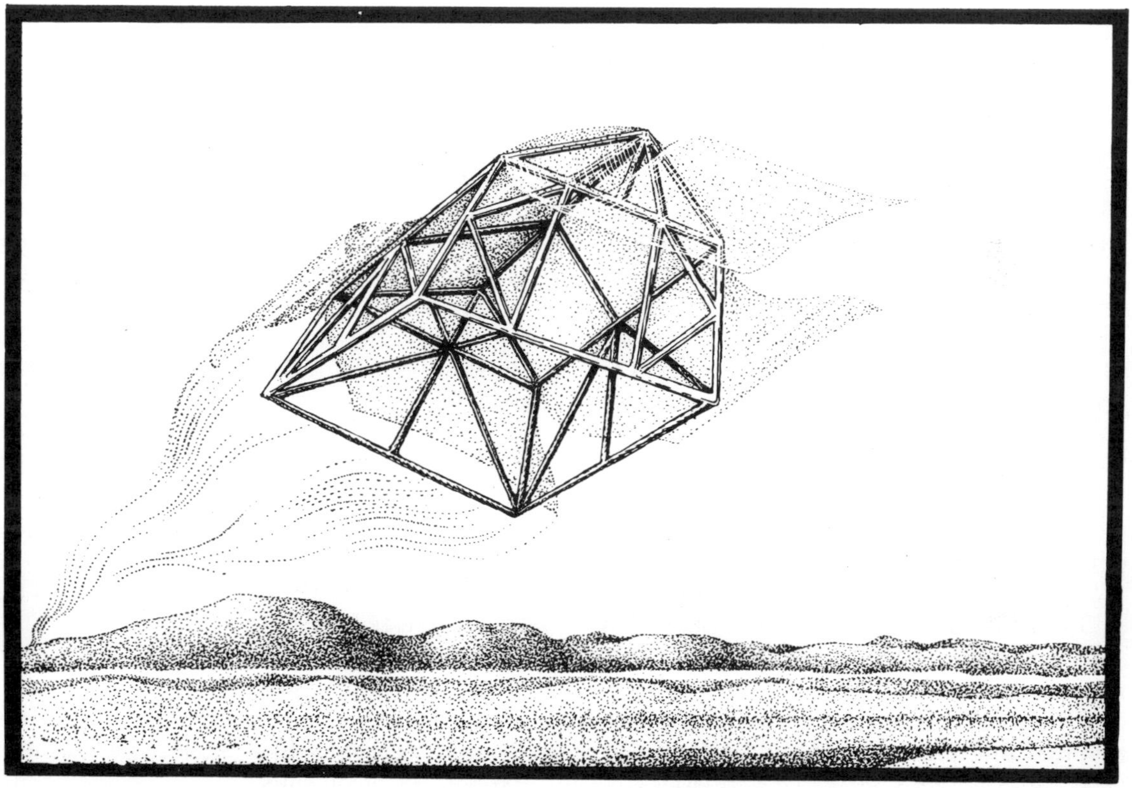

Mr Higgins of Clydebank, Glasgow, purchased a tubular steel greenhouse and, in lieu of glass, covered it with heavy duty, translucent plastic. This done he went indoors.

An hour later his son Stanley came in from playing to say that he had seen the greenhouse flying away over the neighbouring houses. A quick look round the garden convinced Mrs Higgins that the boy was right. When the man next door arrived with the same story Mr Higgins was disturbed.

The family searched high and low for the greenhouse. Eventually it was discovered floating down the Clyde some four miles from Mr Higgins' place.

The Clyde Pilotage Authority said: "We doubt if it is a menace to shipping."

Many citizens of the United States dislike the idea of social services financed either by national or by local government. However, there were no complaints when Rock Quarry, a new prison in Georgia, was declared open.

Rock Quarry, a hygienic stone fort staffed by men with guns and clubs, was designed for wrongdoers whose wickedness had survived both removal from the scene of temptation and the lessons of penal discipline. Beside its white walls was a granite quarry where the convicts paid their debt to society. The method of repayment was by smashing large blocks of granite with 20 lb hammers from six a.m. to six p.m., excluding lunch break. It is a general principle that the richer the society the heavier the burden of a convict's debt.

One day in August forty convicts working in the quarry sat down in the shade of the granite and stretched their legs over the lengths of stone they would be smashing later in the week. Three other convicts moved down the line and used their hammers to break the eighty legs extended before them.

This incident caused a stir.

A State Committee was sent to investigate working conditions and listened patiently to the many grumbles about whipping, starving and bludgeoning.

"All we want is for the beatings to stop," said one convict from his wheel chair. The staff vigorously repudiated any suggestion of unnecessary brutality.

Six months later the State Committee reported that there was nothing wrong with working conditions in the new prison.

As Warden Hubert Smith said: "Like the time thirty of them slashed their tendons – just a stunt to get sympathy."

Clearly, it was a failure.

On Sunday afternoon Martin Dunn walked along Randolph Street in Camden Town absolutely nude and shouting:

"How about this?"

Prominent among the devotions created by members of the Roman Catholic faith are the Stations of the Cross – a series of fourteen images depicting Christ's ascent of Mount Calvary and the various incidents alleged to have happened to the condemned man on his way to execution.

The Stations owned by St Peter & St Paul's Church in Cheshire were rather modest until, in a moment of enlightened generosity, Mr William Brabin, a wholesale food manufacturer, decided to commission a new and more substantial set.

"The spirit moved me," said Mr Brabin.

The spirit in question understood the demands of filial as well as of religious piety, for, with the £650 Mr Brabin gave to the sculptor (a Liverpudlian named Thomas) he included two snapshots of his mother. Thomas was asked to use Mrs Brabin's likeness when he came to carve the Blessed Virgin Mary.

"My mother was a great benefactor of St Peter & St Paul's. In fact she practically paid for it," said Mr Brabin.

When the work was done Mr Brabin gave a party to launch the new series. Many people came and some of them complained that the image of the Virgin Mary reminded them of Mrs Brabin; others remarked that it was a slight on the patron's father; and a few suggested that Mr Brabin should not associate himself so closely with the Son of God.

"Criticism won't worry me," said Mr Brabin. "Thomas has caught my mother's expression beautifully."

"I did not succeed in getting a likeness," said Thomas.

"I am in charge here," said the Reverend Quinn.

"Nobody knows what the Virgin looks like," said Thomas, "and most of the complaints have come from Anglicans."

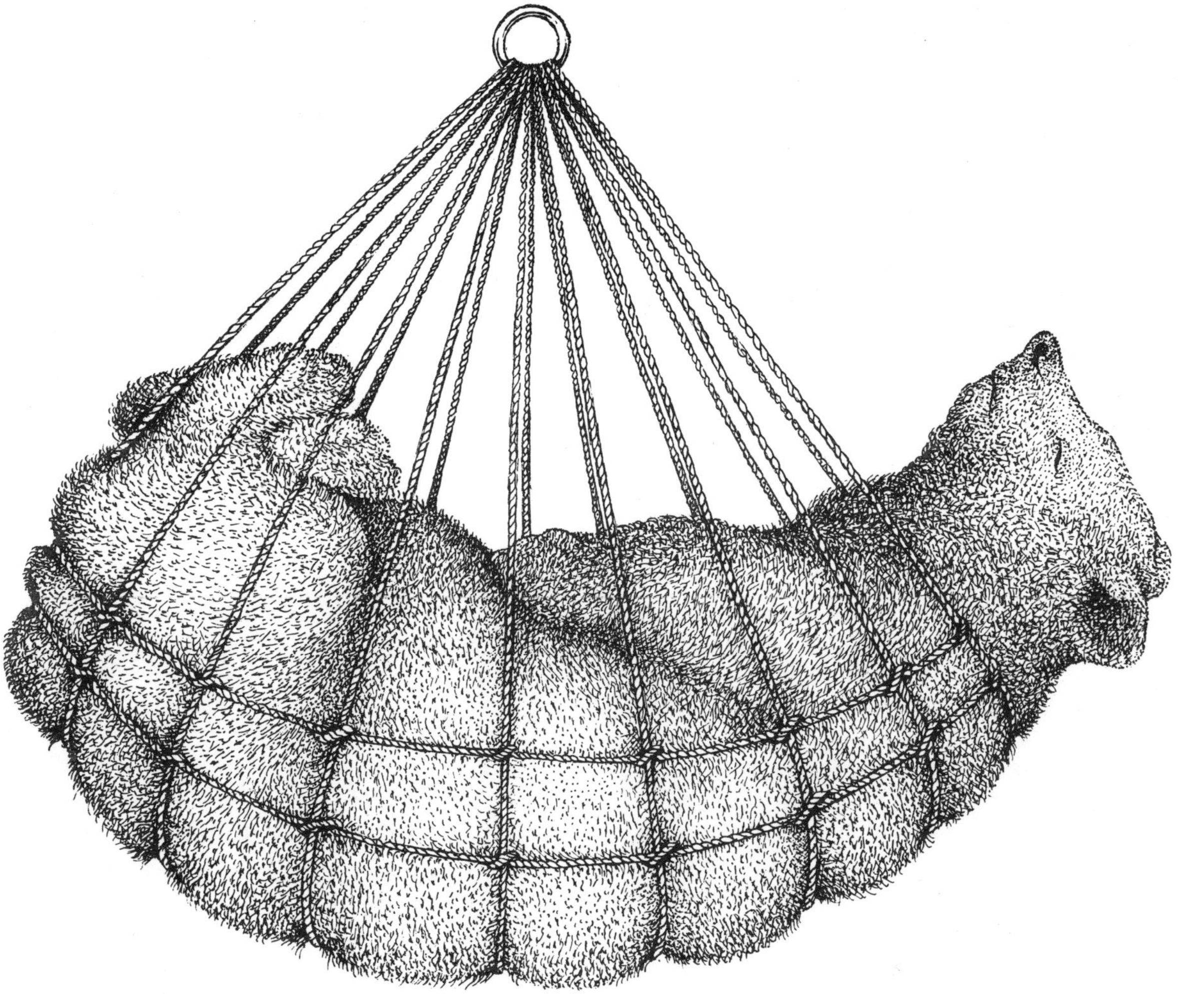

Mr Lynn Rodgers, a graduate game-keeper of St Pauls, Minnesota, has been made responsible for the safety of local bears during their hibernation.

Driving from den to den in his six-gear, eight-track stereo snowmobile, he gives the bears a tranquiliser, weighs them, and takes their temperature.

This treatment assures hunters good sport in the spring.

Outraged by a vet's diagnosis of gross sexual indulgence, Mrs Helen Conway of Bayswater, London, removed her collapsed poodle, Pinky, from his consulting room and went home in a huff.

Next day Pinky died.

An autopsy vindicated Mrs Conway's doubt. Pinky died after choking on a hazelnut.

The North Road Pigeon Fanciers Association, which includes owners from six counties, met at Derby for their annual Grand Release – an event which culminates in the liberation of 20,000 racing pigeons.

At a given signal the birds were launched into the air, the owners regained their vehicles and hurried off home, each one hoping that one of his birds would be the first to reach its loft.

Since that moment not one of the birds has been seen.

"This is the worst disaster in the world history of homing pigeon racing" said the Federation. "We can only assume that the birds ran into a fog and went the wrong way. They could easily be in Austria by now."

Facing Judge Loch and the Criminal Court of Moabit, Mr Karl-Heinz Pawla proceeded to the witness table in order to make a statement.

Once there he took off his trousers and shat on the floor. He furthered his contempt by tearing out eight pages of the Penal Code and wiping his arse with them.

"My only regret," he said, "is that I couldn't reach the judge's hat."

Sentencing him to ten months in prison Judge Loch pointed out that his act was in no way mitigated by his claim to be demonstrating against the existing social order in a natural and spontaneous manner because he "prepared his action with deliberate purposefulness by taking laxative tablets."

Mrs Doreen Chamberlain of Surbiton replied to an advertisement that read: "Two loving and inseparable ginger kittens require a good home." The advertisers were the R.S.P.C.A.

Soon after her application, Mrs Chamberlain was visited by an Animal Home Finder employed by the Society who declared her house to be a suitable place for the kittens to live. Their names, said the Home Finder, were Reason and Tickle.

When the animals arrived, Mrs Chamberlain noticed that they were not ginger, nor were they small enough to be called kittens; she was soon to discover further errors of judgment on the part of the advertisers.

Released from their basket, the inseparables made a bolt for the fireplace and vanished up the chimney.

In the hope of enticing them down, Mrs Chamberlain placed a saucer of milk on the hearth. Two days later she telephoned the Society and told

them that Reason and Tickle were still up the chimney. "Try opening the french windows," said the Inspector.

After two more days Mrs Chamberlain called the Society and explained that the french window strategy had failed. This time the Inspector's attitude hardened. "Light a fire and smoke them out," he said.

This method produced no better result.

On the fifth day the Inspector arrived and dangled a "cat trap baited with juicy kippers" under the flue, and when neither Reason nor Tickle came out, he sent for the Fire Brigade.

Two sturdy brigadiers scaled Mrs Chamberlain's roof and dropped rocks on the cats; after a while Reason emerged from the flue, tore round the room, ripped the curtains to pieces, covered the furniture with soot, and vanished back up the flue.

More rocks drove her back down. This time she made straight for the Inspector and bit him. He killed her. There was no sign of Tickle. "Maybe she went through the french windows," said the Inspector.

Asked for an explanation of their advertisement, the Society said: "As far as we are concerned Mrs Chamberlain was told yesterday these two cats were wild on the night her daughter fetched them from the vet where they were being neutered."

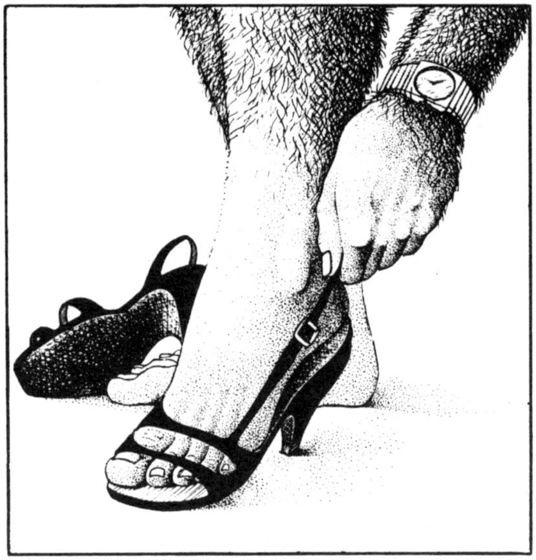

From a letter to the *Calgary Herald:* "As a woman who is married to a transvestite, I want to thank you for pointing out that men who enjoy dressing up in women's clothes are not necessarily homosexual.

"My Bob is all man. He stands six foot two inches tall and weighs 190 pounds. After the children are asleep he puts on high heels, false eyelashes and a wig before slipping into a negligee. I call him my Bobette and we both look forward to these wonderful moments in our life. He is a different person. He even finds the jokes on television much funnier."

When asked why he had opened a night-club in Harlow, Mr Fred Humphries replied: "Well, it's dead – isn't it?"

Aiming at a "Talk Of The Town" atmosphere, Mr Humphries took the Tye Green Community Centre, put in some coloured lights, and called it Chez Don Club.

The bill for the opening night included Bob Monkhouse, two "Top" bands, and a comedian named Phil Ray.

"I saw him work and he was great," said Mr Humphries.

About 800 people turned up.

The first turn was a band called The Shay. They arrived, took a look at the audience, and left: "Our music is very loud," they said.

As the second turn Mr Humphries appeared and announced that Bob Monkhouse was not appearing. "But," he added, "there's some fabulous acts coming on about ten."

He then introduced a disc jockey, D.J. Mark Roman, formerly of Radio London. Seated at his radio-gram, Mr Roman made his opening announcement: "I am not Mark Roman, I am Royston Jay of Discotheque Entertainments – but I have worked for a pirate radio."

By the time Mr Jay had finished playing his instrument, the next band was announced: "We bring you – The Ravers!" said Mr Humphries.

When he had left the stand the band explained that they were not The Ravers but the Harvey Smith Combo. "We agree we are not the band ordered for the evening – but we know Mr Edwards who runs the Ace of Clubs Agency."

Mr Humphries reappeared to say that he had never heard of Mr Edwards or the Ace of Clubs Agency: "Throughout the negotiations I have dealt exclusively with the Johnny Laycock Agency."

When the time came for the comedian, Mr Barry Taylor was announced and appeared; however, Mr Humphries had been expecting Phil Ray – who had gone abroad and had put in Mr Gerry Martin as his substitute, "Nobody knew where Barry came from but he was a great hit," said Mr Humphries.

The audience has signed a petition asking for more shows of the same kind.

Mrs Jolene Gearin of San Pedro, California, told the court: "I am utterly exhausted after spending the inheritance."

Having been left £200,000, Mrs Gearin and her family dedicated themselves to spending.

"We bought a couple of dozen cars, a lorry, £2,000-worth of hi-fi equipment, and a few houses. Then the whole family had their teeth capped, I had my breasts lifted, and we all went to psychiatrists. It has been very hard work. But I will say this for it – it was the first time in our lives that we really worked together."

As part of his Christmas service, the Reverend Don Churchman of St. Jude's, Southsea, Hants, held a conversation about the birth of Christ with Jerry, his ventriloquist's dummy, from the pulpit.

"This is not a gimmick," he said.

Jerry, dressed in a choirboy's surplice, was a big hit. Closed circuit television had to be installed in order that the congregational overflow could watch Don's act from an annexe.

Forty percent of Italians taking their Civil Service Examinations thought Julius Caesar was a type of French Cheese.

Soon after the launching of the Chinese satelite, the Indian Minister of Defence announced that India would be popping one of their own into a low-level orbit within a few years.

Up to now India has been assisted in her space programme by the Soviet Union, the United States, ourselves, France, West Germany and Japan. The greatest height achieved from the Terls proving ground came when a two-stage Centaur rocket reached 150 feet.

Busts of Tenyson, Dickens, Darwin, Faraday, Gladstone and Disraeli, have been stolen from the front of Stanley Hall, South Norwood.

"They have probably been sold by now," said Mr Smith the hall's manager, "there is a demand for that sort of thing nowadays."

John Rodrigues, a Brazilian quarry worker is in hospital, after attempting suicide by throwing a rock into the air and bouncing it off his head.

Arriving at a luxury villa with five cars in its garage, the Spanish police charged its occupant, Senor Francisco Salguero, with obtaining £46,176 from the National Assistance. Senor Salguero, a bachelor, had been drawing welfare payments for 70 children.

The French police have an interest in Senor Salguero, too. They believe he can help them explain the existence of 3,000 imaginary children and their parents on whom the Welfare Francaise spent £2 million since 1962.

Holding an about-to-be-baptised infant in one hand, Reverend Spinney of Meltham, West Riding, dipped the other into the font and felt a "foreign body".

Relinquishing the infant, Reverend Spinney found that three pork chops were floating in the holy water.

"It was an unusual event", he said. "Fortunately the ceremony passed off without further hitch. The chops divided nicely between myself and the two church-wardens."

While removing a fish from his hook, a Chinese angler of Taipel, Taiwan, was surprised when his catch jumped out of his hand, into his mouth, and choked him to death.

"I have always been mad on flying." said Mr Partridge, as he leapt into the morning air off Hammersmith Bridge.

"I think he's an idiot," said his friend, Mr Goyen, as he strapped on Mr Partridge's home-made wings.

"I know they'll work as they are designed on the same lines as Leonardo da Vinci's," said Mr Partridge.

The flight, due at high tide (7.0 a.m.), was an hour and three quarters late because the van bringing Mr Partridge to the take-off point failed to appear.

"It is my intention to glide 50 ft and to land on the bank," he said, poised himself on the parapet, and took off.

After hitting the water his life jacket failed to open and he had to be dragged to safety.

"Next time I will make wings with a 30 ft span and tie balloons on my feet," he said.

"I don't know why?" said Mr Goyen.

"I feel akin to the birds;" said Mr Partridge, "my surname proves it, and my first name is Donald after the famous duck."

Mr Reginald Barnard and Hilda, his wife, packed five suitcases and four bags into their car, followed them in, and drove 150 yards to their favourite hotel, the Grand, in Skegness.

"There is no pleasure on the roads these days", said Mr Barnard. "This way we will not be tired after our drive home."

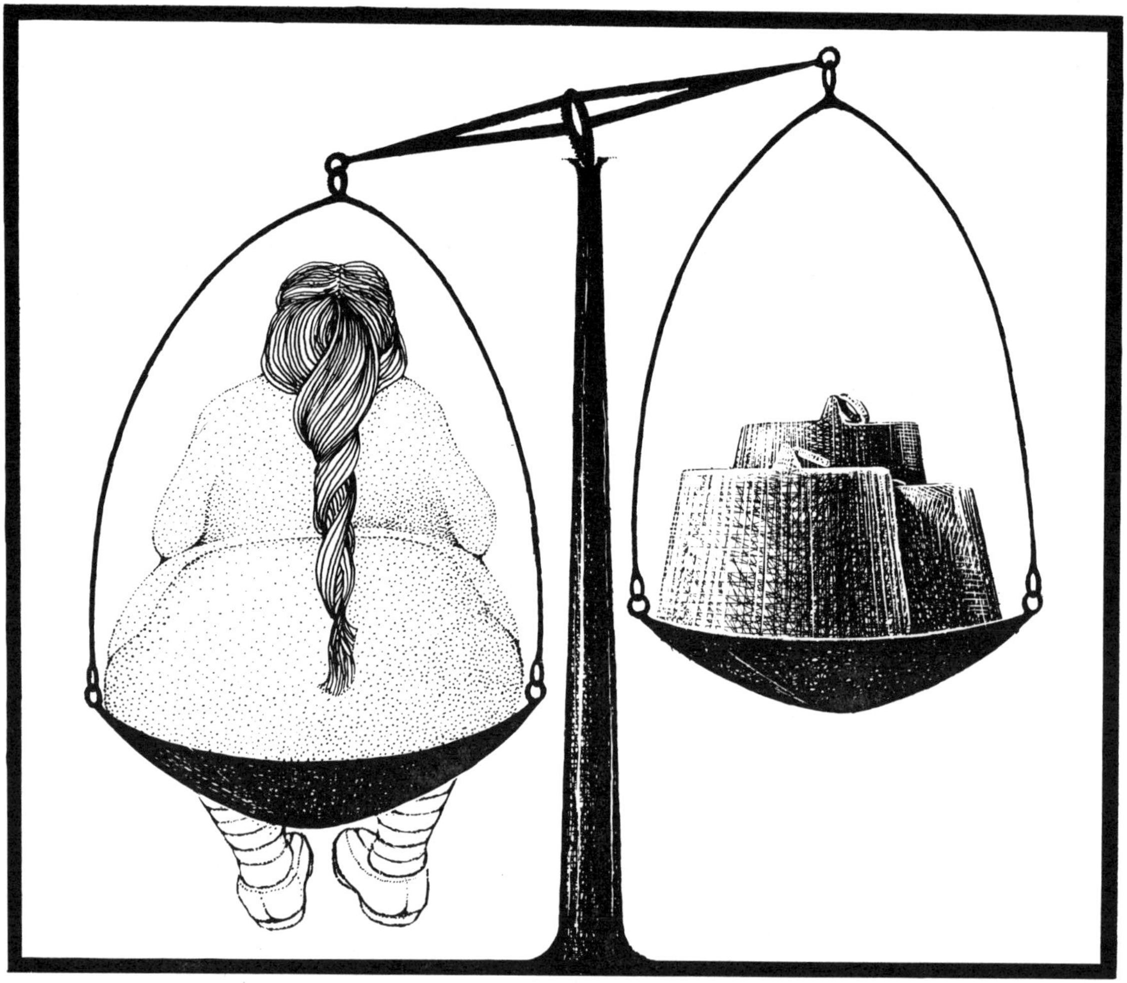

For several months Mr Branislav Radosaljevic, an inn-keeper of Smederovo, Yugoslavia, heard nothing but praise for his wife's beauty from Mr Miloslav Stevanovic, a local cowman.

At the end of one such eulogy Mr Radosljevic offered to sell her to Mr Stevanovic. Accepting the offer the cowman agreed to pay £3 per body weight kilo and, as a token of good faith made a down payment of £50.

The following day the citizens of Smederovo watched while Spasojka, the prize wife was weighed in the village square. She turned the scales at 120 kilos or 17 st. 2 lb.

Realising that he would have to pay a further £310, Mr Stevanovic withdrew from the deal and demanded the return of his down-payment. The inn-keeper refused to give him the money and turned his wife out of doors. The cowman refused to take her in.

"I don't know what Miloslav is complaining about," said Spasojka, "he knows I'm no chicken."

Encouraged by a great deal of advance publicity a large crowd of German, French, Dutch and British tourists converged on the village church in Casamicciola for the wedding of Amelia Eden and Giovanni Borelli.

The merry but impatient crowd became very excited when the local organist took it upon himself to play the *Marseillaise*. They began to sing.

Inside the church things were well in hand: German and Italian photographers shouted abusive remarks at each other in the pulpit, and the police (who had been ordered to calm things down) shouted abuse back; a tape-recorder fell off the pulpit stunning a police sergeant; several spectators were arrested and beaten; the crowd began to boo, and the choir broke into "Ave Maria".

They were no more than halfway through the opening verse when two more busloads of tourists arrived straight from the beach and dressed in bikinis. Determined to get into the church they fought with those who were trying to get out of the church. Several bikinis slipped and three Swedish girls were arrested on the altar for indecent exposure.

At noon the bride arrived and the police began to manhandle the crowd; six Italian photographers shoved their way down the aisle photographing the bride as they went; the crowd went mad with excitement and the police were forced to bludgeon a path through their cheering faces in order to get Amelia on to the altar. The spectators who were struck cried out in pain, but their cries only encouraged those who were being crushed against the walls to cheer more loudly.

The organist played *Here Comes the Bride*.

Lady Eden, the bride's mother, and her friend, Stella Clamp, discovered a tape recorder hidden behind the altar. They ripped it out and were showered with curses by an Italian TV unit who had managed to kick the German photographers out of thc pulpit.

"I cannot let the ceremony proceed unless I can hear what the priest is saying," shrieked Lady Eden.

John Eden, Amelia's brother and MP for Bournemouth West, blushed deeply.

"What has happened to our sweet little church?" said the priest as he rang his bell.

Throughout the ceremony the Borellis and the Edens embraced each other.

The couple were married and went to a nearby restaurant for their reception. Drums, violins, and accordians led them forth. The restaurant was even fuller than the church. Guests crowded on to the balcony 150 feet above the sea. The manager warned them it might collapse but they paid no attention.

At the height of the reception the Bishop of Ischia arrived and, to welcome him, the band played *Colonel Bogey*.

"Let me by, I am carrying the Bishop's ice-cream," cried an Italian waiter – dropping a spoon in the Bishop's lap. The Bishop was not put out; he went on reading a prepared wedding statement two pages long:

"This is a love story," it began.

Lady Eden kissed the Bishop's ring.

In the end the bride and groom were hurried aboard a speed-boat for Naples, leaving behind them a German photographer who was shouting:

"Let me in the boat! I am English!"

Madame Ivy Cannon, a charwoman employed at The Ministry of War, has been given two years' imprisonment plus a £500 fine for covering her jampots with top secret military documents.

The translation of a correspondence between two French army officers:

Commander of Company "A"
To
The Commander of Battalion "T"

Sir,

It is my honour to call your attention to the following considerations vis á vis the consumption of toilet paper by our company.

I have ascertained that we could, without appreciable error, estimate our consumption during a normal period at seventy cms per man per day.

Eight months personal observation allows me to verify this estimate and to describe it as our valid mean average for Officers, Warrant Officers, and Enlisted Men, during the aforementioned period.

As you are fully aware, the military toilet roll (current model) measures forty metres. Consequently, at full strength, our Company consumes one hundred and forty metres per day.

The competent authority is entitled to place seventy-five rolls at our Company's disposition; unfortunately we are far from attaining this desirable figure. Our allocation has amounted to no more than thirty rolls *per quarter.*

It goes without saying that this frugality leads to other materials being used, and that these materials are incompatible with the standards of Military Hygiene, detrimental to the psychology of the common soldier, and injurious to the functioning of our sewage system.

May I beg you to use your influence upon the competent authority regarding this delicate matter, and to see that we receive, within the bounds of possibility, an issue which meets our absolute minimum requirements.

I have the honour to remain your dutiful . . .

The Commander of Battalion "T"
To
The Commander of Company "A"

Sir,

In reply to your letter drawing the Battalion Commander's attention to a problem which, though not of major importance, is, nonetheless, not without importance, it is my honour to give you our conclusions, drawn from a detailed examination of the entire question.

It appears that the deficit verified by yourself is neither as disastrous nor as rigid as described. The rolls are issued by the month and not, as you aver, by the quarter, together with Vim, sawdust, iron-filings, blanco (of three shades), and dustbins, these articles, in spite of what you may think, bearing a relation to your enquiry.

However, it remains true to say that there is a deficit of forty-five rolls. Rather than itemise the various solutions suggested to us, we feel it would be best to appeal to the civic pride of the individual soldier and to the traditional frugality of the average French citizen.

You might care to point out that, to allow the regular consumption of seventy cms, per man, per day, represents a rise of NF 200,000 per battalion per year, should seventy-five rolls per company, per month, be issued.

May we suggest that, out of niceness, your stores might have been subject to pilfering? This could be avoided by issuing toilet paper at morning parade.

In conclusion, and bearing in mind the full facts, allow us to assure you that your issue will be increased to forty-five rolls per month, and that it must suffice.

I have the honour to remain . . .

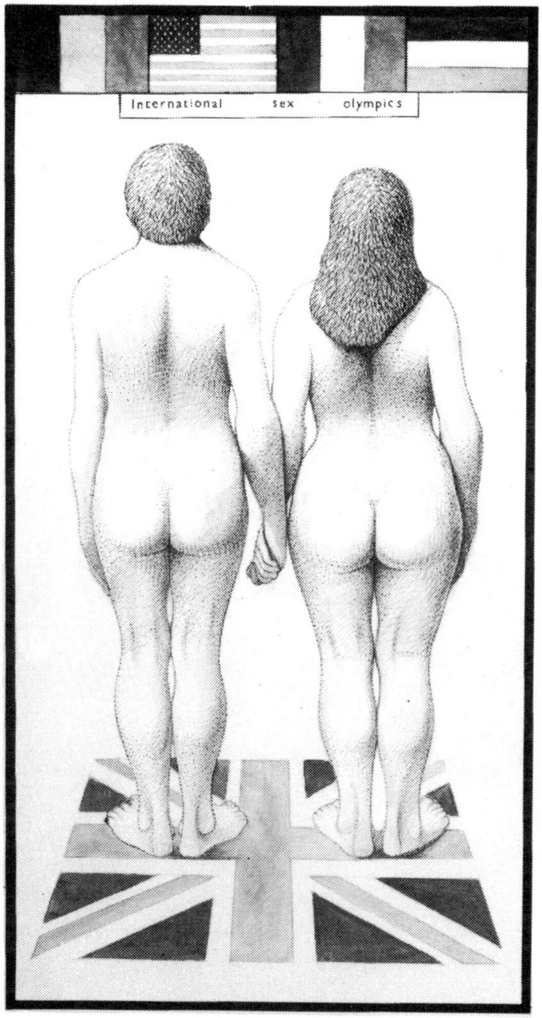

Following the financial success of the closed-circuit heavyweight boxing championship, Dr Harrison Rodgers, a speech therapist of New York City, has devised a Sexual Olympics in which seven heterosexual couples will compete for World Champion Lovers '71.

The seven couples come from France, Italy, China, West Germany, South Africa and England. The British pair – they have invested in towelling gowns charged with a Union Jack – are Mr and Mrs Robert Everett. Selected as finalists from heats involving 47 pairs, Mr Everett said: "We will do our best for our country. We do not have any special training diet. The actual competition will take place on narrow massage tables. Dr Rodgers has said that the response has been staggering. If we win we will take on all-comers."

Dr Rodgers staged the heats in a gymnasium. "Half way through the competition the caretaker entered. He was surprised to see 94 copulators on the matting. However, we gave him a beer and he soon got into the spirit of the thing."

"The great difficulty is," he continued, "to keep the tone high and the Mafia out. As judges we hope to have The Police Commissioner for New York and Hugh Heffner the distinguished publisher."

Asked if he would participate in such a competition, Dr Rodgers said: "Most certainly not. I regard sex as a private matter."

No clipping supports this story, but I have found its source reliable on other occasions.

A world-famous mountaineer was asked to pass the weekend in a grand provincial home. Arriving late and last his hostess enquired if he minded sleeping in the haunted room. He did not mind.

The room was small, remote from the others, beamed, and the bed, into which he climbed after a good supper, a curtained four-poster.

At about three in the morning he was awakened by a slurry, shuffling sound which seemed to come from just beyond the bed-curtains.

Hoping it would go away he stayed put. It got worse. That is to say it became a strangulated series of gasps.

Surrendering to his fright the mountaineer put his fingers in his ears and his head under the bolster.

Some time later the noises stopped and he went back to sleep.

Next morning he drew the curtains and found that one of the maids had hanged herself from the room's main beam.

William Hampshire lived in one room of his mother-in-law's house with his wife, Margaret, and their three-year-old daughter, Eileen.

More than anything else in the world Margaret wanted a home of her own. The chances of her getting it were distant as William earned less than £9 a week.

One day Margaret found a house that would suit their pockets. She told her parents and they gave her £150 for the deposit. "The money they had put aside for their old age," she said.

Taking his daughter and the money William went to the estate agent. By the time they arrived the house had gone.

William felt he could not go home. "I just couldn't face Margaret," he said. Instead, he stopped a taxi and told the driver to go to the West End.

For the next two days William and his daughter lived like kings.

"I wanted to give her a good time," he said. "We're not rich and she's not all that pretty. She may never have such a good time again. I've shown her the sights of London – and not on buses, not on your nelly – it was cabs for us, cabs all the way."

When they got home there was only five pounds left.

"My parents' life savings squandered in two days," said Margaret, "and he wasn't ashamed – not him. He was as jaunty as ever. All poshed up. New overcoat, shoes, tie, smiles – everything. Not a word about being sorry."

"That Bill isn't coming into my house," said her mother, "the doors are locked against him."

"I bought Eileen a gold watch," said William.

"What does she want with a gold watch? She can't tell the time," said his wife.

William was also sacked by his employer.

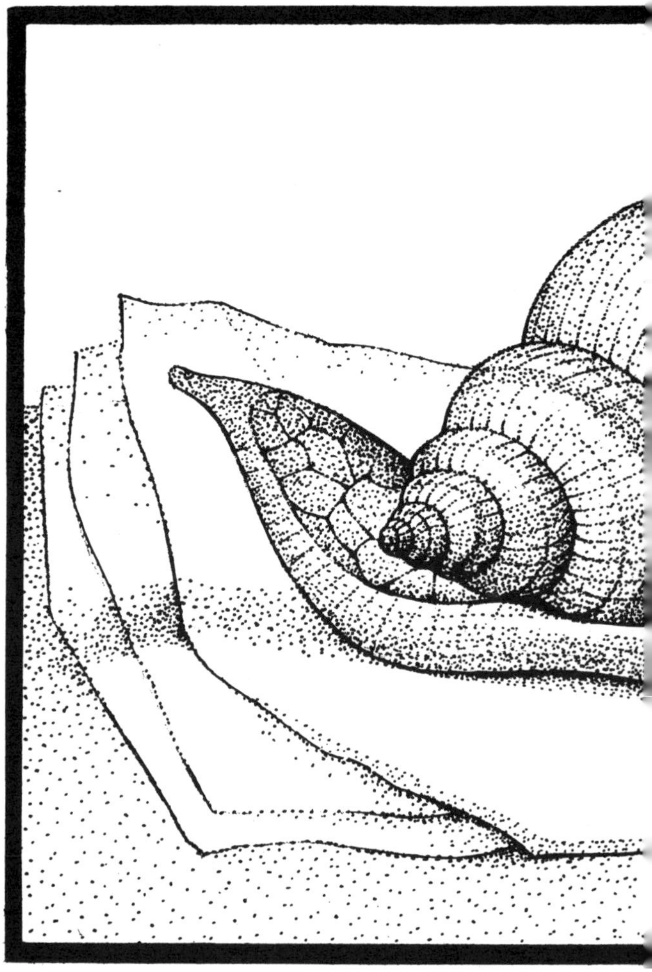

Mrs Doris Honeysett received a tattere
a note from the Post Office explaini

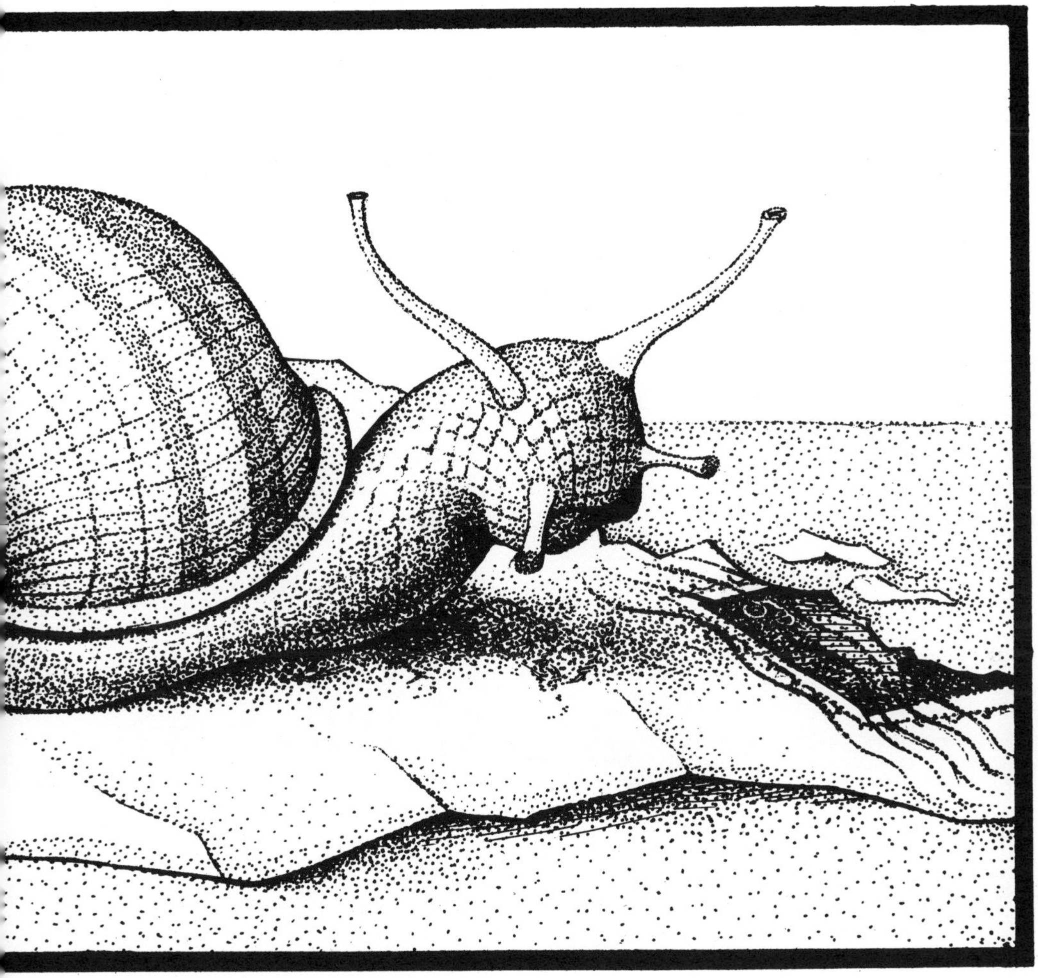

grubby letter accompanied by
at it had been eaten by snails.

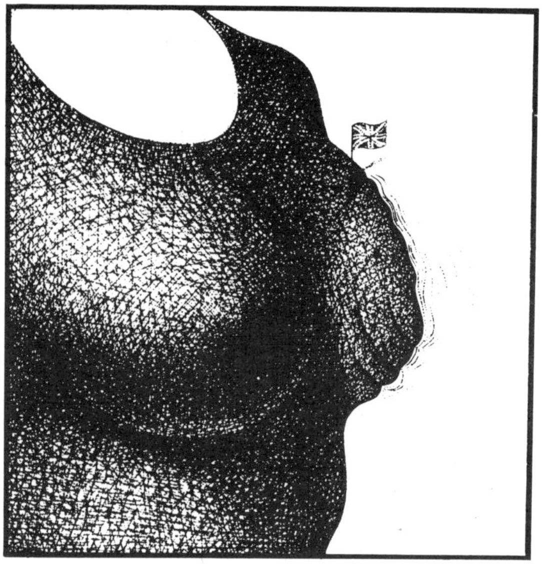

A Maidenhead store is selling inflatable brassieres. A note advises customers not to wear them on flag days.

Rising in the House of Lords, Thomas Coke – alias The Earl of Leicester – said that it was the first time in 22 years that he had made a speech. Public silence was traditional in the Coke family, he said. His father never made a speech in his 23 years as a member of the House; nor his grandfather in his 32-year membership; nor his great-grandfather during 67 years of regular attendance. The Earl spoke on pollution. He said he thought it was a bad thing.

In January Martin Money left his parent's home after a prolonged row. His family and the police searched for him. Finding neither hide nor hair they gave the search up.

Six months later Mr Money discovered his son living up a tree one hundred yards from the parental home. He had been living on fruit and wild birds.

"The whole thing is ridiculous," said Mr Money.

A fire in the caravan of Mr Orlando Romaine, who has been working with the Anglo-Danish Circus, destroyed his bed of nails.

The police at Wendover, Bucks, found Mr Kwan Wee Kwim, a Korean chick-sexer, wandering through the fields at midnight. Arriving from Portugal he had been driven down to Wendover and left in the village. Mr Kwim was hoping to see his employer who lives in Wendover.

"He had failed to make an appointment." said the employer's wife, "so we did not let him in."

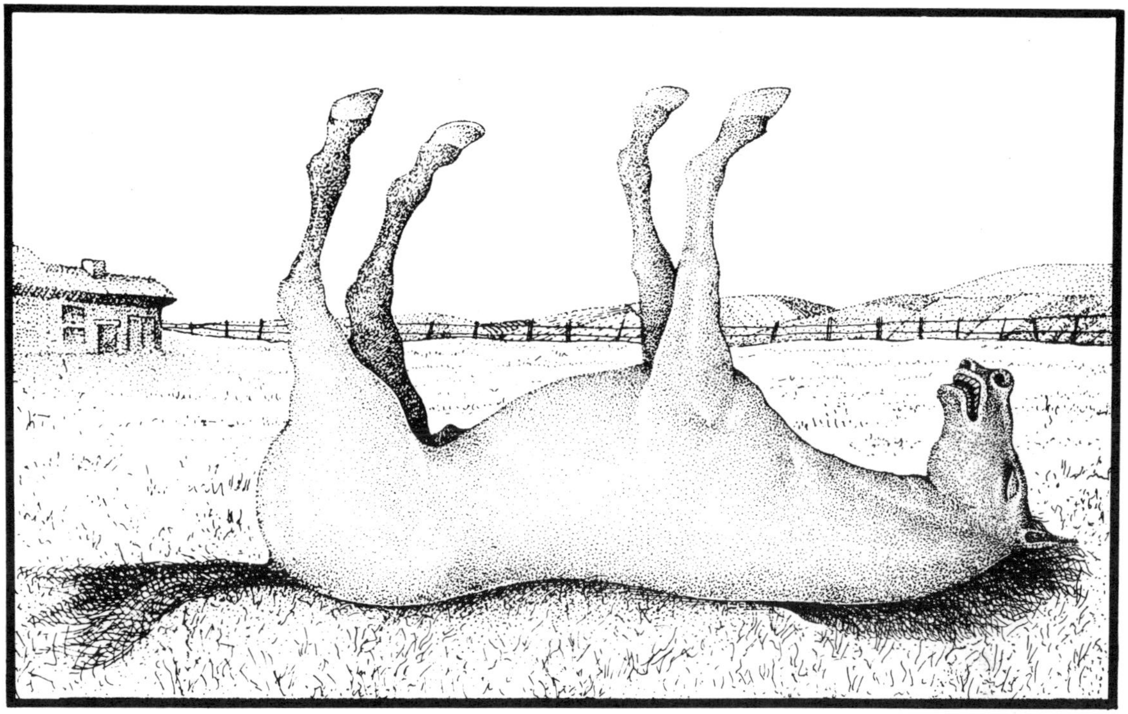

Mr Philip Davis of Farnham, Surrey, owns a gelding called Rodger who is in the habit of sleeping on his back with his legs in the air, eyes shut and mouth open.

This attitude has caused so many motorists to telephone the local police that Mr Davis has erected a large sign in Rodger's field saying THIS HORSE IS NOT DEAD.

Mrs Joan Cooper, a dog-lover from Essex, offered her two Chihuahua pups for sale.

Telephoned by a prospective buyer, Mrs Cooper was asked, "Are they matching?"

"They are about the same size," she answered.

"But," said the customer, "are they the same colour?"

"Unfortunately not," said Mrs Cooper. "One is black and the other is cream."

"Ah," said the customer, "that won't do. We want to use them as bookends – after they have been killed and stuffed, of course."

When Mr Wilson Dinsdale of Hawes, Yorkshire, returned home to his farm, he was surprised to see an Angus cow looking out at him from the bed room window. Reaching the first floor of his farmhouse, Mr Dinsdale's surprise increased when he found his prize Herefordshire bull and a new calf lying across the bed.

"I approached with care," he said, "because I did not want the cow to jump out of the window."

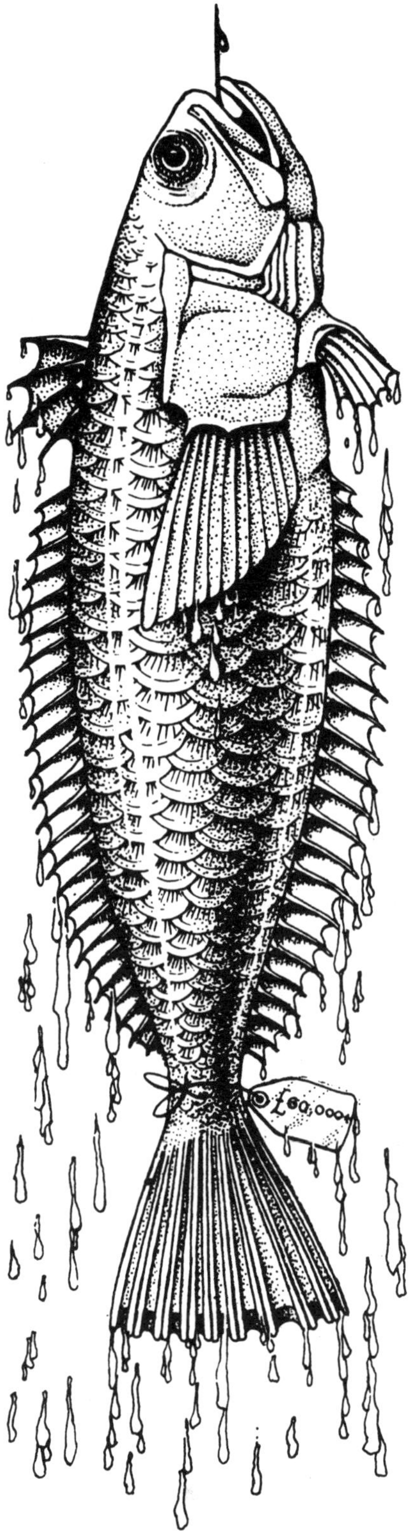

In Poole, Dorset, fourteen-year-old Colin Wilson caught a poisonous weever fish off the quay. He shouted to his parents for help and they, leaping out of their new Austin Westminster, rushed to his aid.

As the Wilson's tried to flip the weever fish back into the harbour, their car began to roll forward, gathered momentum, and ran over the quay's edge, crashing onto *Caledon*, a £60,000 yacht that was just tying up.

Mr Everett, the *Caledon's* owner, said: "I had just cancelled a trip to France after a gale warning."

Having climbed into the sixteen foot barrel of a circus cannon in order to test the firing mechanism, Mr Thomas Pretty of Nottingham shot himself 50 feet into the air and landed in his own garden, adjacent to the fairground.

"My wife was surprised to see me before lunch," he said.

When Mr Horace Fittun, The Professional Projectile, heard of the accident, he said: "I knew that they were going to increase the range of Big Bess to 100 feet, but now I decline to appear."

Mr J. Weston-Webb, the circus owner, said: "If Fittun wants to quit he can. The business is full of unemployed human cannonballs.

"As a matter of fact I am designing a revolver-style cannon which will shoot six of them into the air in succession."

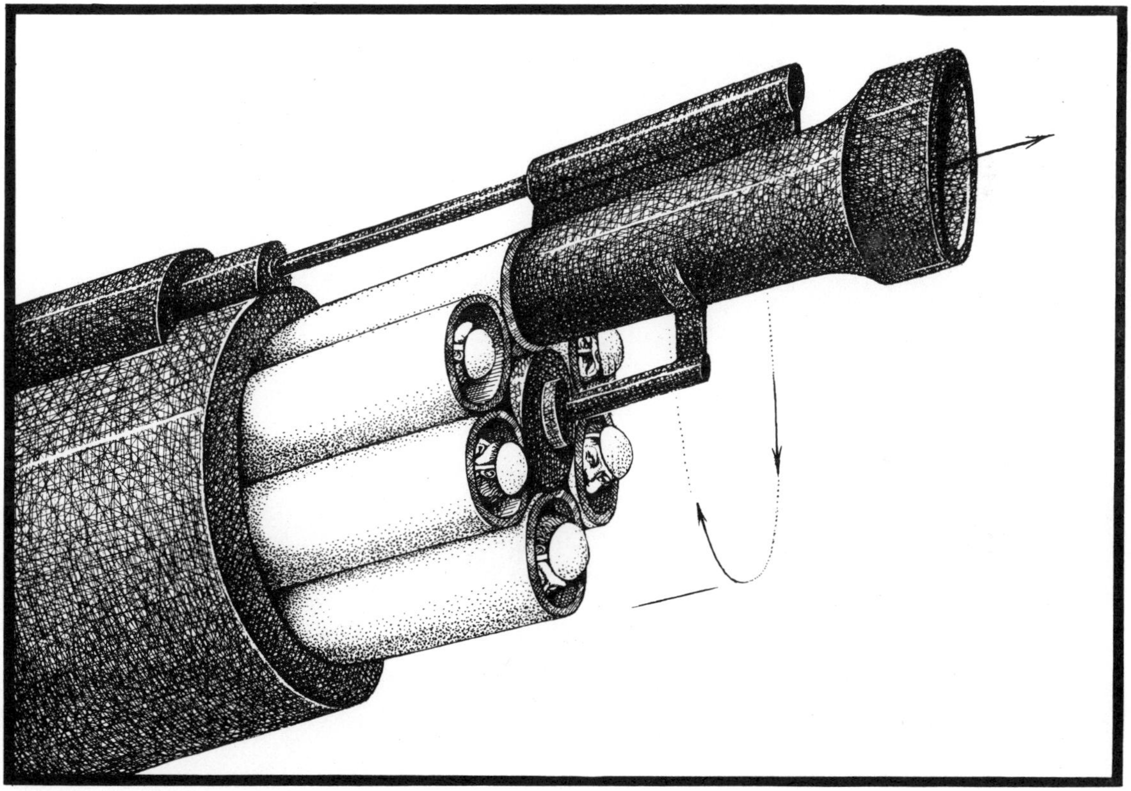

By means of an advertisement Mr Alfred Testo informed the public that he was willing to pay £1 a dozen for fleas. As master of The Hull Flea Circus he felt he was in a position to assure sellers that their fleas would be given a good home. "My daughter, Pauline, allows the fleas to feed off her body once daily," he said.

"There's a shortage of good fleas," said Pauline. "I blame the vacuum cleaner and these new concrete buildings. We've had to manage with Portuguese fleas. It's terrible. There isn't a decent British flea in the show."

Bimbo, a seven year-old elephant who lost his interest in water ski-ing after a car accident, has been awarded £1,750 damages by Judge Turtle of the California Supreme Court.

After being given a report that five "weirdos" were looking "for a river" a Glaswegian member of the Skegness flying squad alive to the constant problem of illegal immigrants, stopped and searched a car containing five Punjabis, one of whom was holding a cardboard box wrapped in a plastic bag.

Asked what the box contained, the man, who could speak only a little English, said "Asheesh".

At the station the box was found to contain the cremation ashes of the passenger's mother.

"After the search", said *Alert* – the local police newspaper – "the police escorted the funeral party to the River Heaven, where the ceremony was completed."

Mr Ernest Law, the proprietor of Mack's Cafe at Alconbury on the Great North Road was sometimes disturbed by rowdies demanding food. To frustrate such visitors he purchased four guard dogs, the largest and most vicious of which was called Tiger.

"Anyone in their right mind who sees Tiger bare his fangs, says *That's it* – and leaves. Last Whit Monday Tiger scared off 50 Hell's Angels," said Mr Law.

He had not reckoned with Mr Ifor Williams, a horse dealer. Finding Tiger gazing at him in a nasty way Mr Williams bent down, picked him up by his forepaws and bit his ear off.

"It's nothing unusual," he said, "I often do it to quiet horses down. That's the language they understand."

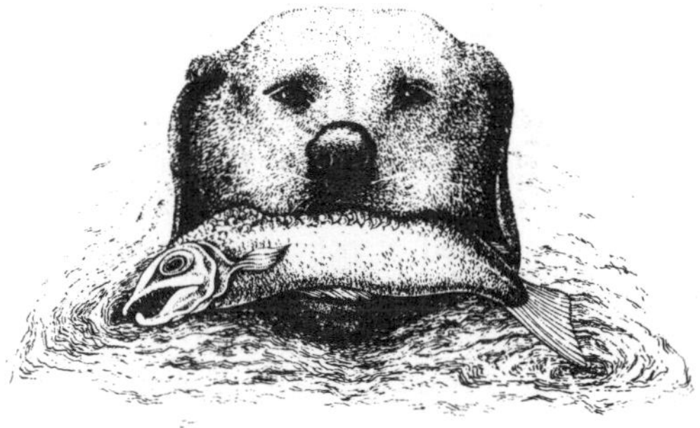

During a walk along the banks of the River Severn where it passes Shrewsbury, Randy, a labrador owned by Mr Eric Titly, leapt into the stream and emerged with a 9 lb salmon in its mouth.

Hardly had Randy regained the bank when Mr Titly was approached by an Inspector from the Severn River Authority who seized the fish in the name of his Office.

"This fish must be thrown back into the river," said the Inspector.

"The fish is dead," said Mr Titly.

"In that case it should be buried," said the Inspector.

Later, the Authority announced that the salmon had been placed in a deep-freeze and a receipt issued to Randy.

"If one dog is allowed to go fishing, pretty soon half the dogs in the country will be up to it," said an Authority spokesman.

THREE SMALL ADS:

1

A small familied, disabled ex-serviceman, 63, widower, pensioner from World War One, wishes to dispose, urgently, of a modest agricultural business, 2 houses, 5 hectaires (4 hectaires vine, 1 hectaire fruit), new agricultural machinery; and wishes to contact an ex-serviceman with a view to marrying his only daughter, 23, beautiful, pure, past irreproachable, affectionate, hardworking, thrifty cook, homebody, has given every satisfaction to her father (whom she agrees is a man of honour), would prefer an ex-serviceman, 25-30, of good character, presentable, fit, some savings, set on marriage, handy about the house, non-smoker, non-drinker, past irreproachable, experienced tractor driver, some knowledge of vines, possessed of other agricultural and manual skills (bricklaying, for example), enabling him to find useful employment during slumps (because of the lack of specialists), send photo; first exchange of letters between fathers only, or other ex-servicemen able to vouch for the honour and loyalty of the applicant; after choice, introduction by father or friends of the applicant to the daughter; may take her out; if agreement – rapid marriage; this will allow me to retire; I am looking for a household companion, ex-serviceman, same age (63), if possible, calm, devoted, pensioned, handy about the house, all costs shared, his wife to keep the house, men share leisure, a gardener, some mechanical knowledge, love of country outings, hunting, bowls, of absolutely no political opinions whatsoever, in need of rest, wife to provide marriageable daughter with good advice, affection, and help, prefers household without children, agricultural worker or small holder acceptable, serious enquiries only; in both cases application by letter.

Nonconforming, curious, or flighty persons need not answer; enclose ex-serviceman's card.

2

Co-pilot, 42 (looks 37), really *very* good, partner in profitable divorce, exceptionally intelligent, will marry magnificent civil-servant, beautiful & intelligent face, minimum height 5 ft. 8 in., slender, curvaceous, having splendid buttocks, conditions must be rigidly adhered to – otherwise useless.

3

Shepherd seeks mountain – in Jura if possible.

Signor Franco Boretti, the owner of Blackie, a mongrel, both living at Port Venus, Italy, has been given two fines of 67p because of the dog's "obscene act in a public place".

"I resent Blackie being branded as a play-dog by the gutter press," said Signor Boretti on the courthouse steps.

"It is quite true that he had the pharmacist's poodle bitch twice in fifteen minutes on the steps of the Convent of St. Mary, but as he has had almost every bitch in Port Venus over the past three years, I don't see what is so special about a manky poodle dog".

Blackie's aptitude has cost Signor Boretti the pharmacist's friendship: "We had played dominoes together for close on sixty years", said the 82-year-old postman. "What does he expect me to do? Show Blackie the two fine tickets? As for having my animal fixed – I would rather go to Russia."

A youth, locked in the lavatory of an hotel in Scunthorpe, attracted the owner's attention by playing *Abide With Me* on a violin for forty-five minutes. "It's my only tune", he said.

"I was having a shave when there was a loud swishing noise followed by a great thud," said Mr Chris Elkins of Addlestone, Surrey.

"My wife and I went out into the garden and saw that our lawn had been seriously dented by a massive lump of ice that had fallen out of the skies."

After some time the police arrived, took it away, and stored it in their refrigerator until someone realised that it was a block of frozen urine jettisoned from a passing aircraft.

"What with the number of aircraft about," said a police spokesman, "we are very lucky it wasn't something worse."

While expressing his admiration for the size of the aircraft and the skill of the pilots landing at Orly Airport Michel Durand, a keen plane-spotter from Melun, blew his false teeth out of his mouth and onto a luggage trolley passing beneath the Observation Terrace.

The trolley continued on its way and in next to no time M. Durand's dentures were airborne.

In his consternation M. Durand failed to notice the aircraft's number. His wife, who was with him, said: "I was reading a book when it happened. I hope this experience dampens his enthusiasm for spotting. Half my life is spent at airports."

Darius Giraud, an ornithologist from Toulon, spent many hours in learning how to imitate the cries of rare birds. While practising in the woods near his home he was shot and killed by a hunter.

It is the custom among the Persians to grant a condemned man his last wish. Another humourous belief of this ancient people is that the felon who dies while making his audience laugh goes straight to Heaven.

A knowledge of these traditions would have subverted the indignation of almost any Western tourist entering Sepah Square, Teheran, and joining the contented mob of 20,000 who had been patiently waiting for the dawn at whose crack Mr Housang Amimi and Mr Safar Rahimi were due to hang.

An interested murmur disturbed the crowd as the two multiple killers were led towards the gallows; children were held up; ladies periscoped their compact-mirrors.

At the foot of the simple machine Mr Rahimi cracked:

"O Citizens!" he cried, "beware of evil thoughts. See where they have led me!"

This failed to get a laugh; he swung to only modest applause.

But the 20,000 had not passed a night of discomfort in vain. Mr Amini mounted the gallows with dignity. He called for, and he was handed, a microphone.

"All in all I killed 24 men, women, and children," he recounted, lighting a cigarette. "I have no regrets to express and no will to make."

Then he sang bawdy songs to the audience, straightened up, and was dispatched – microphone in hand.

The crowd were delighted. They pelted the gallows with money and roared:

"The singer is dead! Justice has been done!"

No documents support the following story. However, its air of surreal loving-kindness smacks of the truth. If my friend, my friend's brother, and I have been deceived, let me be first to congratulate the author of our deception.

Some weeks ago (my friend said) his brother was involved in a car accident, a minor affray in which nobody was seriously hurt, though the hospital insisted on his staying overnight.

In the morning he found himself lying beside a patient whose head and shoulders were swathed in bandages. After breakfast these two began to chat and, because the bandaged man seemed quite perky, my friend's brother thought nothing of asking how he came to be in hospital.

The patient paused: "It's a bit odd," he said, "and I won't blame you for not believing me, but what I'm telling you is the truth.

"Last night I was in bed with the wife and we're just about to make it, see? Going along very nicely we were, when she says: 'Darling, there's someone downstairs.'

"I told her not to be daft. How can there be anyone downstairs, I said? If there was anyone downstairs, Rex – that's our big alsatian – would have 'em in a jiffy."

'There's somebody downstairs,' she said, 'and you can't go on until you've had a look.'

"So up I got – starkers – and went to have a look.

"Sure enough there's a noise coming through the letter-box – one of those slots set in the door-frame, because the door itself is made out of glass.

"Not wanting to open the door I got down on my hands and knees to have a good listen – and maybe a look. I did this very quietly to be on the safe side.

"Well, while I'm listening, the alsatian comes up behind me and licks my behind. I'm so surprised I dived right through the glass – spwam! So I land up here.

"Silly, ain't it?"

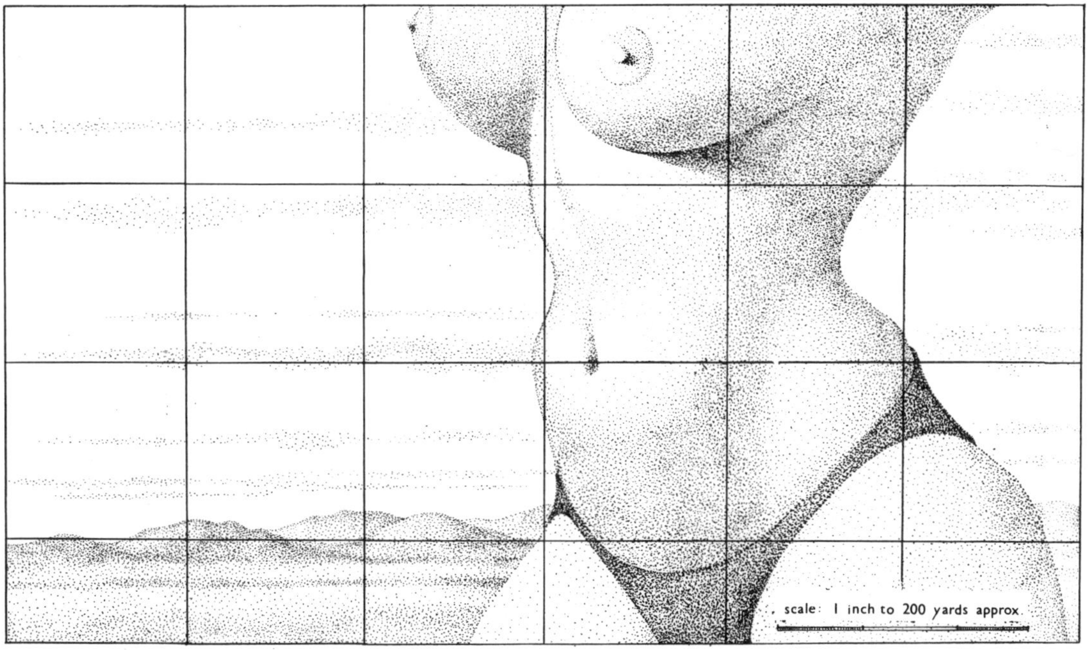

Five eminent statisticians have calculated the collective measurement of the models who have illustrated the pages of *Playboy* magazine since its inception eighteen years ago as: one supergirl weighing 17 tons, with a chest measurement of half a mile.

While touring Italy a group of young English musicians were approached by a Roman promoter who offered them £200 for a one-night-stand; they agreed, albeit reluctantly, to his condition: that they appear in the nude.

The promoter explained that they were to perform before the membership of Southern Italy's largest nudist colony, and, as their audience was not well informed about modern music they would include several old nudie favourites like *"I'm In The Nude For Love", "In The Nude".*

Come the night they were driven to the colony, stripped off backstage, and, guitars appropriately held, made an entry before a large and very serious crowd of middle-aged citizens in full evening dress.

Both parties were furious, especially the band, when they discovered they had been billed as "The Nudie Blues".

When Miss Claudine Perot accepted a part in "Paris – its Nights and Its Secrets", a melodrama, she agreed to be tatooed.

"Standing naked in front of the camera for four hours was very painful," she said. "When they were finished I had the images of a rose and the Eiffel Tower needled into my bottom."

"However," she continued, "after the filming was over, the producers arranged for the tatoos to be removed by surgical graft. That was much worse. I had to lie on my stomach for fourteen days."

Surprise was added to pain when Miss Petot discovered that her employers, Cinematographie Ulyssees Productions, had sold the tattoo to a collector.

Offering to show the court her scars Miss Perot was awarded £2,500 damages, and the tattoo.

In 1956, Mr Warwick Kerr, an Amazonian bee-breeder, decided to combine the attributes of the active but hostile African bee *(Apis mellifere adansonii)* with that of the lazy but honey-gathering Surry Buzzer *(Apis mellifere johnsoni)*.

Before his tinkering was done a swarm of modified African Buzzers managed to get away. Sixteen years later this strain has taken over most of northern Brazil and all of Columbia. It combines great sloth with implacable hostility, is a honey-eater but not honey-gatherer, attacks anything that moves, secretes a poison more deadly than a coral snake, and has already killed numerous mules, pigs, cows, and ten humans.

"The new bee could generate a social problem for infant mothers in Mississippi." said a spokesman for the National Academy of Sciences. "We are planning a sizeable appropriation to create a bee-Maginot across the Panama bottleneck, softpoisoned, heavy foragers, laced with omnivorous sex-scents. The Brazilian modification will be wrapped in a genetic barrier and peacefully experimented. Heading our operation is Mr Kerr."

Each Saturday morning the Rochdale Fire Brigade scrub down their Station with some forty gallons of hot, soapy water.

After being taken to see a vet, the elephant belonging to a travelling circus was diagnosed as constipated and ordered an enema.

The Brigade was willing to help. A brass nozzled hose was connected to a pump, inserted, and the enema given.

The elephant, disliking the treatment, bolted five miles down the road with the nozzle in position and the pump trailing far behind.

Interested readers should note that this story originally appeared in *Pigeon Racing News*.

Certain local politicians who wished to discuss the future of Cumbria, a new–but not yet established–county in the north of England, met at a council of local authorities.

The object of this meeting was to elect a provisional joint committee, a prototype of the true joint committee that will rule Cumbria – if and when Cumbria comes about.

At the outset of the meeting three men were nominated for the provisional committee: Colonel Dickenson of North Westmorland Rural District Council, Mr Dawson of Sedbergh Rural District Council, and the Reverend Oliver of South Westmorland Rural District Council.

A vote produced the following result: Dawson 4, Dickenson 3, and Oliver 3.

At this point a representative from the North Westmorland Rural District Council said that this gave more votes against Dawson than for him. Another vote was taken. The result was: Dawson 4, against Dawson 6.

At this point of the meeting it was decided that Dawson had been eliminated, but that Dickenson and Oliver were to be allowed "a second chance".

This fourth vote produced: Oliver 5, Dickenson 5. However, when the Chairman, Mr Simpson of Windermere Rural District Council, was asked to use his casting vote to settle the matter, he refused, saying that he had not been assigned such a vote at the beginning of the meeting.

In the ensuing silence Alderman Long of Kendal Borough Council said that the way Dawson had been done out of his provisional general joint committee office was "disgusting".

A fresh proposal suggesting that the original vote by which Dawson had been elected should be allowed to stand was accepted. Unfortunately this proposal was defeated 5-3.

This was followed by another proposal: that the meeting be abandoned. This proposal was passed unanimously.

While using the still surface of Lake Rannan, North Borneo, as a shaving mirror, Mr Buthar Singh, an Indian travel agent, was surprised by a freshwater turtle who seized him by the nose and dragged him under the surface.

Recovering from this assault in Sandakan General Hospital, Mr Singh said: "It was an act of God. My father warned me never to shave myself, but I had to do it to please the tourists."

A State beauty queen having accepted an invitation to Hollywood fell into melancholy when she found herself unknown after two years of bit parts.

Deciding to take her own life she travelled by bus to the outskirts of the city and climbed a ridge of hills along whose summit the local Chamber of Commerce had erected in thirty-foot high neon and steel letters, the word HOLLYWOOD.

Reaching the top of the letter H she tuned her radio to appropriate music and stripped to its rhythms. When she was naked she threw herself off.

Instead of landing on the rock she fell into a huge cactus bush, upon whose thorns she lay impaled for three days before she was found, taken to hospital and died.

Two years ago Mr Lewis Matthews of Bournemouth stole a water cooler from, so he said, a man who owed him money.

Released on £25 bail Mr Matthews failed to appear in court on the appointed day. Instead, he fled to Cyprus together with his wife and three children. Cyprus was Mrs Matthews home; she had been threatening to take her own life unless she could live with her mother.

On his arrival in Cyprus Mr Matthews applied for and got a job in the Lebanon. However, soon after he landed there he got into trouble with the authorities and had to move on.

He went first to Syria and then to Turkey – where he was arrested for spying. While in captivity he went blind. In spite of this disadvantage he managed to escape from his prison and, while under fire from border guards, he swam from Turkey to Greece.

Mr Matthews admitted to stealing the milk cooler, which he sold for £2.65. He received a fine of £25.

The Jerusalem police have prevented a Frenchman from crucifying himself on a hill just outside the town.

"There is no room for stunts like that around here nowadays," said a police spokesman.

The martyr said: "I have had myself crucified in seventeen different countries. I think it is a disgrace that it should be stopped in the place of its origin."

Seven poets were bruised when, during an international verse festival in South West Macedonia, a firework representing Shakespeare's head exploded and caused the horse drawing the cart on which they had been drinking to bolt.

An Ottoman beggar, Mr Mahmut Karakucuk, suffered a nervous collapse on finding that his savings, some 4,800 Turkish liras, had been eaten by a rat.

The body of a man dressed in a pinstripe suit with an umbrella under his arm has been found sitting in a crevice halfway down a cliff near Land's End. He was facing out to sea.

Police fought a hand to hand battle with 300 long haired baboons, near Berbera, in the Somali Republic. Both groups suffered injuries.

A report issued by the Ministry of Food states that in a three year seabed walk a crab covered the 150 miles between King's Lynn, Norfolk, and Whitby, Yorkshire. Subsequent to this feat it was eaten.

Mr Jeremy Rodale, a 72-year-old Health Food multi-millionaire, editor of an Organic Gardening and Farming magazine, owner of a 600-acre experimental non-chemical-fertilizer farm, and consumer of up to 70 supplementary food tablets daily, collapsed and died while explaining his recipe for good health on a coast to coast television programme.

Travellers on the 3.20 express from Newcastle to London were surprised when, having assured a fellow passenger, Reverend Robert Middlemiss, that they would not be stopping at York, he fell onto his knees and began to pray for the train to slow down.

Their surprise turned to amazement when it did, and, after apologising to them for any inconvenience he might have caused, the Reverend Middlemiss opened the carriage door and jumped out.

"I was booked to address the British Sailor's Society in York," said Vicar Middlemiss, "I did not want to be late, I am a firm believer in the power of prayer."

A spokesman for British Rail said that Reverend Middlemiss had contravened a bye-law.

Having enjoyed a trampoline act on the television, Bobby Yeomans of Birmingham decided to imitate the performers using his parents' bed as equipment.

After a few sturdy leaps, Bobby – aged three – sailed through the bedroom window onto the lawn.

His condition was described as "excellent".

After the Prime Minister of Australia, one Mr McMahon, had been pelted with jelly-babies in the town of Perth, secret service agents collected the evidence, arrested fifteen assorted rowdies, and prior to charging them, returned to guard their leader while he addressed a crowd of several thousand voters.

When everyone had gone home they returned to base and released their catch.

"We could bring no charges," said a secret service spokesman, "because the evidence had been eaten by Bozo, a cockatoo."

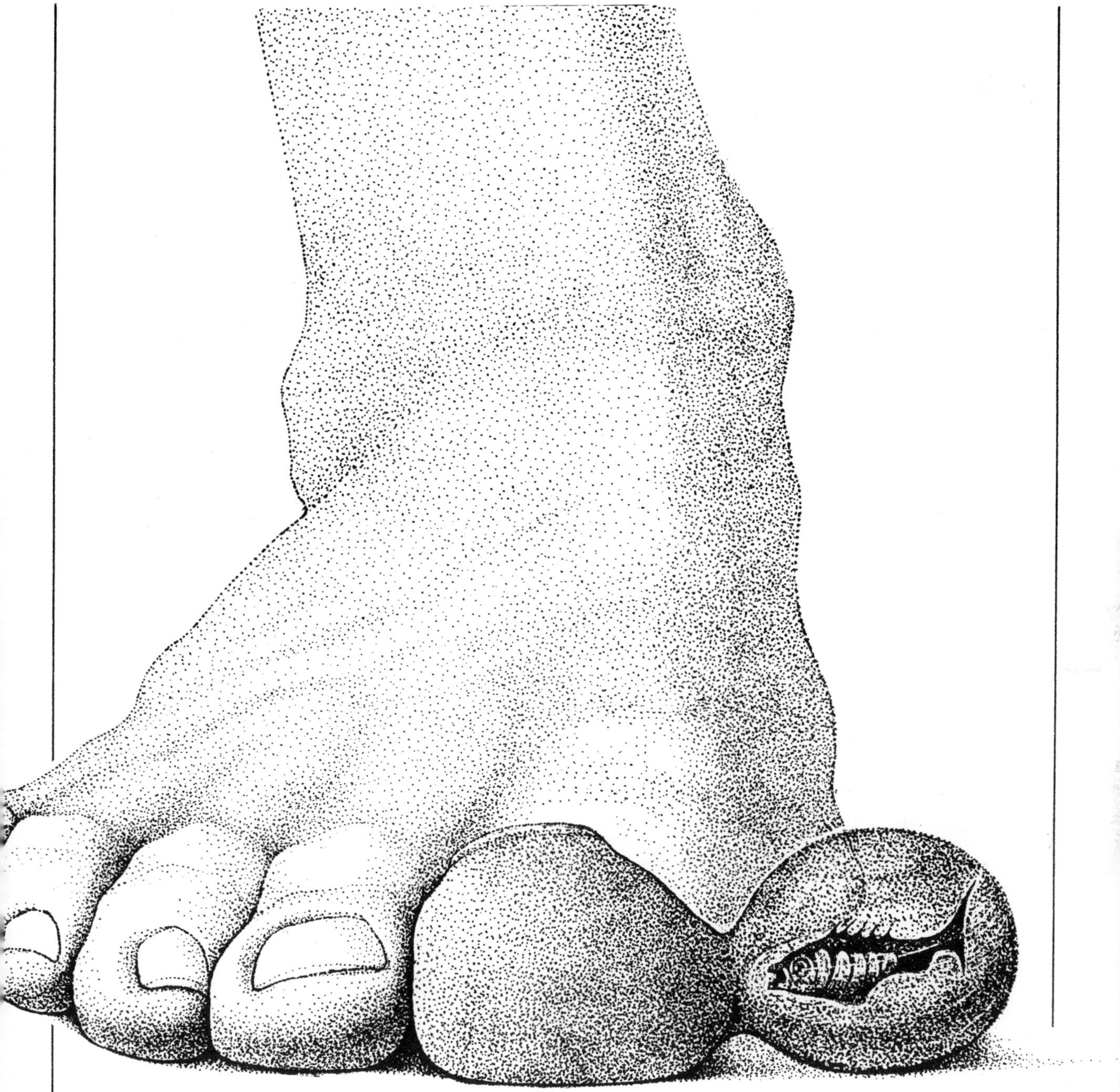

Five weeks after he cut his foot while paddling by the shore of Lake Moondarra, Australia, Mr. David Palmer, a Brisbane fishmonger, developed a very large blister over the hurt place. The surgeon who lanced the blister found that it contained a live, half inch long fish.

Wearing a two tone mini-kilt and dragging a 250lb organ behind him, Mr Kenneth Campbell of Sutherland, is making his way up the side of Ben Nevis.

This is his second attempt to scale the mountain with a musical instrument. The first attempt failed when the grand piano he was pushing ahead of him crashed over a low precipice and dragged him 100 feet after it.

"I was so disappointed when it crashed I went straight home, harnessed myself to the organ and started off again," he said.

Mr Campbell expects to take a week to gain the summit. Each morning, after sleeping the night beside his organ, he breakfasts off porridge, plays *These Are My Mountains* and sets off. When last seen he was well above the snowline.

"I'm doing it all to aid cancer research," he said.

Answering a charge of cruelty against his dog Prince, Mr Sean Wilby assured the court that he did not intend to hurt the animal when he bit it.

"Prince and I do a trick together," he said. "When I go: "Gerrh!" "Gerrh!" Prince crouches down. When I shout: "Oops!" Prince jumps up in the air and I catch him in my mouth.

"To describe it as cruel is nonsense. I do the same with children."

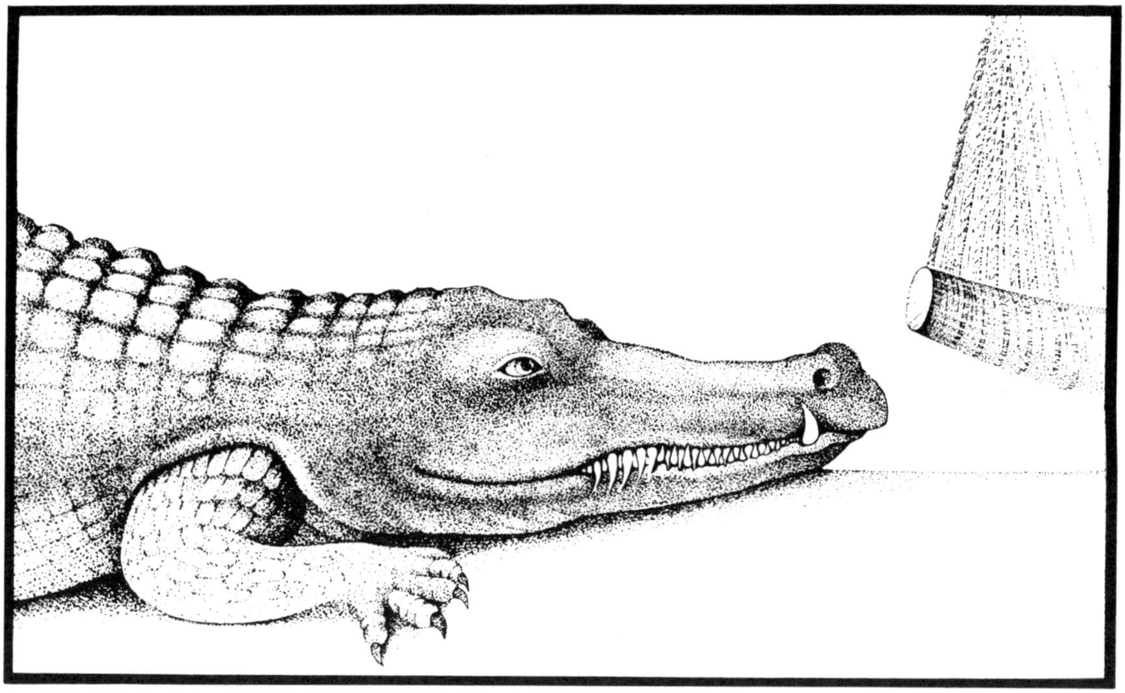

Before going to prison, Mr Shimeon Rimovsky of Tel Aviv asked the magistrate if the court would look after his crocodile.

When the magistrate asked him why he kept the beast, Mr Rimovsky said: "I practice hypnotism on it."

As part of a serious attempt to resurrect their former passion, Mrs Magda Friederich of Munich purchased a Pinkie-Winkie Seethru Babydoll Nightie with which she hoped to arouse her husband on the night of their 27th wedding anniversary.

Mr Friederich, a dentist, showed his appreciation. Thereafter, his wife developed an almost sacred attachment to the colour pink.

The following day she bought a two-piece pink suit with matching suit and gloves; to this costume she added a pink hat and handbag; soon afterwards she limited herself to pink make-up.

At first Mr Friederich said nothing; but when his wife introduced pink wallpaper, pink carpets, pink napkins, tablecloths, dishclothes, curtains, towels, chairs, electric light bulbs, and would tune the colour set to an overall pinkish glow, he decided to speak.

Mrs Friederich would not be deterred. She responded to his complaints by buying pink pots and pans, and, late one night, she dyed her own and her husband's clothes Petunia Roseblush.

Her final gesture was to bring the pink into his surgery where she dyed the surgical chair Musk Blush Winter Poppy.

"I'm just mad about it," she said. "I'm going to be divorced in pink."

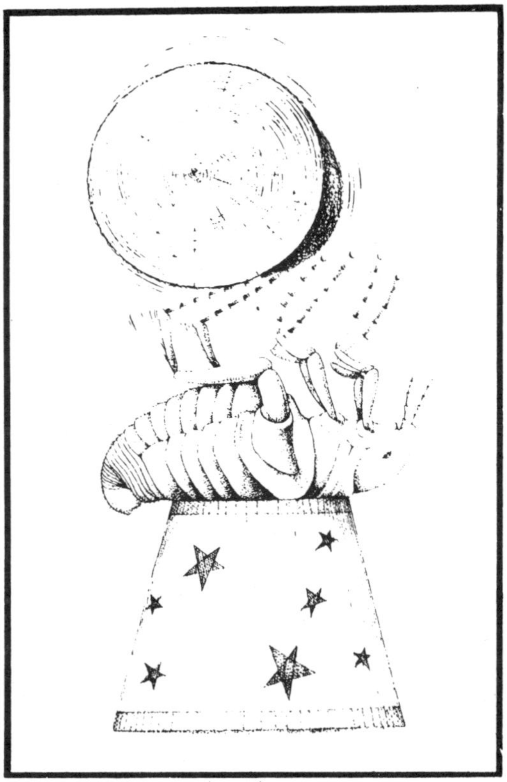

During a performance by Professor Tomalin's Flea Circus at the Midland Steam Fair, a gale force wind struck the tea-chest on which they were giving the show and several of the cast were blown away.

"We've searched everywhere for those fleas," said the Professor. "Some of them are just trash, of course, but how can we replace the star of the show, Fo Fum, the juggling flea – one of the Hot Shots, a group of seven imported from France?

"Fo Fum was the highspot. He used to balance a log twice his size on his hind legs."

Mr and Mrs Pirta lived with her father in a small village two hundred miles from Helsinki.

The parent was elderly – seventy-two years – and it was his wish to be cremated when he died. Realising that his daughter would be tempted to forgo the cremation on account of its expense, the old man added an escrow to his will obliging its beneficiaries to cremate his remains or lose the inheritance.

In due time he died, and Mr and Mrs Pirta fulfilled their obligations to the corpse. However, as an economy measure they thought they would dispense with a coffin.

Dressing the dead man in his best they made their way to the nearest station and bought three tickets (two return, one single) to Helsinki – the nearest town with a crematorium. They boarded the train, placed the corpse on the seat between them, and settled down for the long journey to the capital.

Gradually the compartment filled. Their fellow passengers reacted agreeably. After a time one lady suggested that, as there were people standing in the corridor who might well enjoy the seat occupied by the corpse, it would be sensible to move it on to the luggage rack.

Mr and Mrs Pirta thought that this was a reasonable suggestion, and, helped by the other passengers, they popped her father up on to the rack. No sooner had they done this than lunch was served and everyone went forward to the dining-car.

Travelling by the same train, though in a different compartment, was a heavy drinker, the kind of man who expresses his hostility to his fellow humans through aggressive generosity.

Passing along the corridor towards the dining-car the drinker noticed the corpse on the rack. He entered the compartment and insisted that it shared his bottle.

Naturally, he was ignored – a form of behaviour difficult for sociable drunkards to abide. So great was his annoyance that he dealt the corpse a blow on the head with his bottle before he settled himself on the seat opposite.

Still he was ignored. His anger matured into anxiety. Overcome with self-pity he entreated the corpse to forgive him, to be his friend. When he realised that the old man was dead, he panicked.

Sliding the corpse off the rack, he opened the window and pitched it on to the tundra. Then he fled down the train.

Well fed and fortified against the remainder of their trip Mrs Pirta returned to the compartment and found the corpse missing. They fetched the guard, explained their position, persuaded him to stop the train and telephone to Helsinki. When the train arrived it was surrounded by police.

The drinker, believing himself to be a murderer, gave himself up and begged for mercy. So relieved was he to find that this was not the case that he paid all the crematorium's expenses.

The railway denied all responsibility and threatened to prosecute the Pirtas for the illegal transportation of perishable goods.

Shortly after refusing to pay 47p for the breakfast he had consumed in a Birmingham cafe, Mr Francis Whelan, an 86-year-old pensioner, was arrested.

The next day he refused to be released. "Anyone who has had to struggle along on a pension would be mad to leave Winson Green Prison," he said. "It's a real treat. Three square meals a day, central heating and plenty of new faces."

Mr Whelan rejected bail and remained in prison for three months.

"His is a unique case," said Mr Sime, the Recorder, "in all my experience I have never heard of the prosecution applying for bail on the part of the accused."

"I was hoping to stay in for Christmas," Mr Whelan said. "They say it's very, very good. Unfortunately I'll just have to find a room somewhere."

Mr Whelan's incarceration cost nearly £400.

"Why should I worry about the taxpayer?" he said. "I fought in two wars and worked all my life. If I'm not a taxpayer, who is?"

Mr Whelan was described by a Social Worker as "both rational and intelligent."

Mr. Felix Perez, head of the experimental surgery department at the veterinary faculty of Madrid University, has invented a set of steel dentures suitable for cows.

"Once a cow is fitted with a full set," said Dr. Perez, "its life span will be extended, its sex life will improve, and its milk production soar.

"For as little as £7 a pet lover will be able to grant a new lease of life to his toothless dog. What is more, a formerly sterile animal will in all probability become potent again when fitted with our new rustproof teeth."

The traditional relationship between piety and violence was revived recently at Lourdes.

Among the many believers dipping themselves in the spring was Egon Vosswinchel – a former member of the Afrika Korps. His prostrations were unusually fervent: each and every year he passed sixteen weeks on his knees before the springs; no holy nook, cranny, niche, or pond, popular among the devout, was too obscure for him to visit.

To the citizens of Lourdes, Egon Vosswinchel was a godsend; living as they do from the manufacture of relics, they were not too slow to feed his devotion with accounts of holier and rarer places of local worship. A man such as he, they said, should on no account miss The Cross of Glory – a massive concrete idol sited on a hill over-looking this hive of religious industry.

The Cross of Glory was the property of a French millionaire, Roger de Letoile. Having built it he abandoned his family, raised a hovel beside the hill-foot, and devoted his life to prayer and humiliation.

Vosswinchel was eager to visit the hermit and his totem.

On reaching the site he could not find the holy man but the cross was unmistakable. Without more ado Vosswinchel prostrated himself before it.

His meditations were interrupted by a sharp kick on the rump; there behind him stood the hermit and author of the kick who, instead of joining Vosswinchel's religious activities, ordered him to leave immediately.

After an hour of mutual abuse the penitents separated; de Letoile retired into his hovel, Vosswinchel – outraged and revengeful – to Germany.

Twelve months later he returned. In addition to the prayer-books, rosaries, scapulae, and other superstitious paraphernalia, Vosswinchel carried a rifle.

That night he pitched his tent beside the idol. When the humiliated millionaire awoke from his cold sleep the first thing he saw was Vosswinchel using his cross to make contact with the supreme being.

The years of humility snapped. Screaming and cursing the hermit rushed at the pilgrim; the pilgrim fired at the hermit – and missed. A moment later the two Christians were at each other's throats; they bit, clawed, booted, ripped, and spat on each other. As they rolled down the hillside the rifle broke in two. The hermit grabbed the barrel, the pilgrim kept the butt.

Offering up his feelings of outrage to the supreme being Vosswinchel clubbed de Letoile to death beneath the cross he had built and on whose plinth he had carved: "Peace On Earth".

Among the customers refreshing themselves in The Optimist, a public house in Southampton, was Seaman Fish.

After two hours steady drinking Seaman Fish developed a migraine.

"Like a bubble in my head," he said.

Taking his two companions aside Seaman Fish proposed something in a low voice. They nodded.

Seaman Fish asked Mrs Mallon, a lady with whom he had been drinking, if she would wait. Then the three men left the room.

Outside in the yard the first man searched for a nail, the second found a large piece of wood; Seaman Fish bowed his head and his friends hammered the nail into it.

Everyone came back inside and resumed drinking.

"I didn't know him from Adam," said Mrs Mallon. "Imagine my surprise when he showed me the nail sticking out of his head and said he discovered a new headache cure."

"Once it was driven home I felt much better," said Seaman Fish.

A police spokesman said: "There is no question of black-magic being involved."

Public transport was the means chosen by Mr and Mrs Sayers to reach the Bird Show at Olympia. With them they took two tropical fish housed in a glass bowl.

On the way to the nearest request stop Mrs Sayers felt a need to relieve herself, and, leaving the tropical fish in her husband's safe keeping, she entered a lavatory owned and operated by Harlow Urban District Council.

Admitted by a penny she satisfied her need, but when she tried to open the door the lock jammed and Mrs Sayers found herself immured in the cubicle.

She remained calm.

After some fifteen minutes, during which she applied the obvious and proper means of attracting attention, i.e. beating on the door, screaming, leaping up and down, Mrs Sayers' composure gave way to anxiety.

It was January. A cold day. Buses were infrequent. Her fish were accustomed to warm water.

Almost in despair Mrs Sayers placed one foot on the seat, seized the pipe with her left hand and the lintel of the door with her right, raised herself up, and, to keep balance, put her other foot on the toilet roll. There she paused.

After a few seconds she concluded that the feat of climbing over the lintel was not within her performance. As she tried to regain the ground the roll rolled and Mrs Sayers fell.

She remained immured for several hours and the tropical fish died.

Allowing her Appeal against Harlow Urban District Council, The Master of The Rolls found the Council negligent but the damage suffered too remote to fall within Hadley v. Baxendale, 1859 Ex. 341, though the Council's advancement of Adam v. The Lancashire Railway Company, 1896 L.H. 4C.P.739, 'a minor inconvenience countered by a major risk,' was not an acceptable contention.

Photographs of the lavatory were handed round.

Solicitors: Messrs Kitkat & Whisker.

A ship of 7,000 tons sailing from Malmo to Bornholm was run ashore on the coast of Sweden by her Captain. "The reason is simple," he said. "I was drunk".

In the course of a long and intensive political debate, the Windemere council's Health and Parks Committee decided against the enlargement of the Rayrigg Meadow Car Park.

A proposal by Councillor Birchall to enlarge the 30-car park to a 100-car park was narrowly defeated.

An amendment to decrease Councillor Birchall's figure to 60 cars suffered the same fate.

A further amendment to the amendment of Councillor Birchall's original proposal, i.e. that the park should contain a maximum of 50 cars, was also defeated.

Councillor Dr Oakden's proposal that there should be no extension whatsoever was treated with derision.

After a cup of tea, Councillor Miss Carter proposed a park for eighty family cars "as a compromise". This proposal was heavily defeated.

The Council Surveyor, Mr Jack Connell, said: "If the area is developed to too great an extent, the natural beauty would be lost."

Everyone agreed with this.

Councillor Lubbock said that he hoped the matter would be decided before Rayrigg Meadow became part of Cumbria "so that the people will have something left to enjoy".

Summing up, Councillor Birchall said that people with cars should be given as much consideration as people with boats, and deferred the matter of the car park until the next meeting.

A proposal to hand over any decisions about the size and siting of nine new Picnic Tables to the Pier and Lake Committee was passed unanimously.

Senhor Michaelangeli Phuta of Belem, Brazil, was arrested for entering a cinema with Dolores, his pet Boa constrictor, around his neck. Senhor Kaukmann, manager of El Stella, Belem's only cinema, said: "The snake was under age".

Senhor Phuta said: "Dolores goes where I go. We had been looking forward to *Gone with the wind* for six years."

While her husband is away on Territorial Army manoeuvres, Mrs Alfrieda Boggie is assuming his "stay-put" position among the boughs of an 80-foot elm, threatened with felling by Newark Borough Council.

An executive from one of the oil companies was detailed to watch the behaviour of potential customers when faced by self-serving petrol machines.

One lady arrived, got out of her car, read the instructions, and inserted a £1 down the nozzle of the hose. Finding that nothing came of this she shouted: "Five gallons of regular," down the same nozzle. After that she left in a bad temper.

She was followed by a man who wrote his name and address on a piece of paper and popped it into the slot designed to take £1 notes. Asked why he was doing this, he said: "It said *Insert a note* so I did."

Since 1923 The Sons of Freedom, a Doukhobor sect practising in Canada have, in the name of God and the cause of peace, killed twelve humans, bombed 44 schools, fired a hospital and eight churches, burned down 22 of their own villages, blown up 54 railway lines, destroyed four post offices, three theatres, 19 sawmills, and a Greyhound bus depot, started eight major forest fires, and flooded a jam factory.

Recently the Canadian Government awarded the sect a grant of $25,000 with which to build a centre for the study of Doukhobor Culture.

A twenty-six year old woman went to the Central Police station at Ndola, Zambia, to report a man who had threatened her with a pistol.

She made her statement to Constable Phiri.

She was about to leave the station when the Constable said that he found her very attractive and would like to make love to her. He offered ten shillings for her services.

She replied that this was insufficient; however, when he increased his offer to fifteen shillings, she accepted.

They went upstairs to the main lecture hall where, to her surprise, Constable Phiri stripped himself, and requested her to do likewise.

Her engagement had not been completed when the door of the lecture hall was opened and Assistant Commissioner Humphrey Nthere of the Zambian CID, accompanied by a class of trainee detectives, entered.

The Assistant Commissioner explained that fornication in the main lecture hall was forbidden.

Without looking up, Constable Phiri said that he was very busy taking a statement and would they please come back in ten minutes.

Facing the magistrate, Mr Frank Lifuka, Constable Phiri said: "So far as I know there is no rule against fornication in the station. I paid to satisfy my desires, and I removed my uniform out of respect."

Subsequent to a weight decreasing operation, Miss Jane Pepler of Johannesburgh turned brown. Her mother said: "It is heart-breaking to see Jane spurned because she has become Coloured, and it is particularly embarrassing for us because we are strong believers in white supremacy."

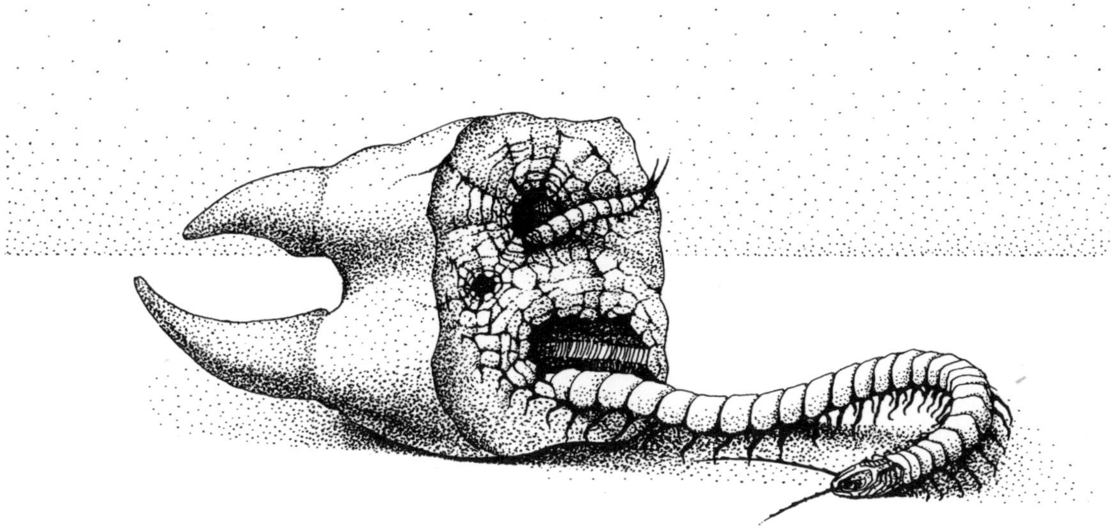

When Mr Barnet Kopkin, a dentist of Stoke Newington, had pulled one of Mrs Ruth Abraham's teeth, a centipede uncurled itself from within the tooth and walked around his operating tray.

"It may have been there for quite some time," said Mr Kopkin. "Such events are unusual, of course, but I once had a patient in whose mouth a tomato seed had begun to grow into a small plant."

August P., a Viennese old-age pensioner, loved and was loved by his dog, Schnauker.

Schnauker was a very fat dog, and while August P. felt no aesthetic distaste for Schnauker's obesity, he was alarmed for his health.

August P. decided that his dog lacked proper exercise. This lack came about through August P's teeth – which were missing. Without teeth August P. could not whistle. Without whistling he could not attract Schnauker's attention. Unless he could attract Schnauker's attention August P. was reluctant to let him off the leash.

Drawing £10 out of his saving's account August P. made his way to a dental surgery situated on the top floor of an apartment house near his home.

In the hall of the apartment house he met Alois, the caretaker.

"I'd better come up with you," said Alois, "the lift isn't too reliable."

Half way up the shaft the lift stopped and the light went out.

"It must be a power-cut," said Alois.

Reaching into his pocket he produced a deck of cards and a candle.

"We can pass the time by playing," he said as he lit the candle, "these power-cuts sometimes last as long as two hours."

August P. agreed and lost all his money. Then the power came back on.

Filled with despair August P. entered the dentist's waiting room and told his story to the two patients who were before him. They said the same thing had happened to them.

"Surely a man of your age knows better than to play cards with a total stranger?" said the magistrate.

"I agree, your Worship," said August P. "But I'm afraid of the dark and he said he'd put out his candle unless I played."

The borders of Assam and Burma are formed by the Lushai hills. Perched along the spine of these hills and isolated from each other by deep valleys filled with bamboo jungle, are a number of villages belonging to the Lushai, a warlike tribe, whose predatory nature caused their neighbours much distress until they were disarmed by the British Army and indoctrinated by Baptists.

After these defeats little was heard of the Lushai until, in 1959, a deputation formed of village elders appeared in Bombay to inform the government that many of their people would be dying of starvation in 1961.

They were asked why.

Because the bamboos will be flowering, they said; and went on to explain that the bamboos flower only once in 50 years, and that the last time this occurred many people died.

The governors told them not to believe all they were told and sent them back to the hills.

In 1960 the bamboos flowered. The rats who shared the hilltops with the Lushai ate the flowers and multiplied prodigiously. Next year there were no flowers so the rats ate the Lushai's crops. When the crops were gone both the rats and the Lushai began to die of starvation.

The government had no foodstocks; the villages were too small for planes to spot and drop supplies; the Lushai could not meet in one space because the valleys are too narrow and, in any case, were packed with starving rats; neither jeeps nor tanks could climb the steep hillsides. Many people died.

Third time lucky – and the bamboos will be flowering in 2009.

Mr John Whitedriver, of Santa Anna, California, has been arrested for sharing his caravan with a donkey, 3 grizzly bears, 13 dogs, 3 rabbits, an ocelot, a bobcat, 9 chickens, 2 opossums, 3 peacocks, 16 quail, 5 pigs, 5 doves, 6 pigeons, a monkey, a woman and 8 children. He has been charged with cruelty to animals.

Twelve months after they had installed a television set in her home, a firm of electrical suppliers received a call from their customer in the course of which she explained that the set was keeping her awake at night.

When an engineer arrived at the lady's house he asked her if she had tried turning it off.

"I did not know that you could switch it off," she said. "The picture is excellent, but after a year I do feel in need of a rest."

A new magazine *Instant Cookery* features the following recipe among its 25-second puddings: "Take a can of peach-halves, spread with raspberry jam, sprinkle with dessicated coconut, serve on slices of chocolate Swiss roll."

For ten years Louis Ralui was employed as The Human Cannon-Ball of Chipperfield. Five times a week his wife fired him out of their cannon and during his professional life he was hospitalised seventeen times.

"Now I'm retiring," he said, "my wife's aim gets worse and worse. In Belfast she shot me straight into the arc-lamps and I bounced off into the lion's cage and broke my neck. It was the last straw."

The litter bin at Kessingland, Suffolk, has not been emptied for 15 years. It is still only three-quarters full.

Invited to attend an arts festival devoted to singing and dancing, the ochre-daubed warriors of Okapa, New Guinea, were so surprised when the judges failed to award them the first prize they fired their bows into the audience of jet-set tourists.

Without more ado the attendants, who were riot police in disguise, charged the stone-age tribesmen. The Okapa warriors stood their ground. It was not until the tourists joined forces with the police that the performers were overwhelmed and chased back into the jungle.

In love with his neighbour's daughter, Mr Dorsun Yilmaz of Dalmali, Yugoslavia, organised an elopement.

Soon after midnight, his beloved, wrapped in a blanket, descended the ladder he had placed by her window. He carried her to the car and away they sped.

Five miles down the road he unwrapped his treasure and found that he was carrying the girl's grandmother, who beat him up.

The police in Salisbury, Rhodesia, were obliged to arrest a naked white man who walked into the bedroom of a young couple and climbed into bed with them.

The man, who analyses marijuana samples for the Royal Canadian Mounted Police Crime Laboratory in Alberta, was called Mr Joynt.

Entering a Johannesburg boxing ring, Mr Roy John, a Welsh light-heavyweight, confirmed his reputation as a dead-pan wag. When he removed his dressing gown the audience were astonished to discover that he had forgotten to put on his shorts.

His opponent in the bout was a Mr Arno Prick.

A £100 limited edition of *The Rhyme of The Ancient Mariner* has been published by Mrs Josie Holton.

Restricted to 100 copies, the poem will be printed on seven varieties of seaweed. "This is my first attempt to produce a book printed on seaweed," said Mrs Holton. "I used edible seaweeds only. If you get fed up with the book you can always eat it."

Mr William Borthwick and Mrs. Florence Pierson, aged 75 and 61 respectively, have been fined £40 for running a blue film service for old age pensioners in Southend, Essex.

Explaining his lack of attention at the wheel, Mr Ronald George of Stroud informed the magistrate: "My mind was preoccupied by the thought of my grandson who is in hospital with a broken thigh, my brother who is seriously ill in another hospital, my wife, who is caring for my eighty-eight year old mother-in-law, and my sister who has collapsed under the strain of looking after her – to say nothing of the stress involved in the reorganising of local government."

Mr Gene Roberts, a legless Vietnam war veteran, abandoned his attempt to swim the Channel after two hours in the water. He was accompanied by Mr Richard Freeman, a blind advertising man from Banstead, Surrey.
The pair navigated by listening to the sounds of a gramophone screwed to the transom of a preceding dinghy filled with friends and well-wishers.

A prosperous driver found his way blocked by a cyclist. Both vehicles were halted outside a large Police Station. It was noon; some hundreds of people were watching.

The prosperous driver sounded his horn. The cyclist (a Postman) ignored this warning. The driver eased forward and knocked the Postman's bicycle to the ground. The Postman stood looking at it – amazed. Then, collecting his wits, he turned towards the car and shattered both headlamps with the cap of his boot.

The driver alighted from his car, removed the cigar from his mouth, and jumped up and down on the footman's bicycle, damaging it seriously. The Postman stood back with his hands on his hips.

Neither man spoke.

When the driver was back behind his wheel the Postman raised his boot and put it through the car's spot-light.

Once again the driver descended; he walked over to the bicycle, stooped, raised it above his head with both hands, and dashed it to the ground. He returned to his seat.

By now the road was clear.

The driver moved his car over the bicycle, crushing what remained of it. As the car went by the Postman slammed his knee into the door, denting it badly.

The crowd dispersed.

No one emerged from the Police Station.

An Australian lady driving her two young sons from Sydney to Melbourne found the road surface inferior. Thinking that she had taken a minor road she decided to push on and hope for the best. In any case it was pitch dark. She felt safer in the car.

A few minutes later the front of her car struck something like a tree.

Getting out to investigate she found she had driven half a mile into a coal mine. She and her sons emerged six hours later.

Mr. Rhys Llewelyn Jones, the Flintshire coroner, recorded a verdict of accidental death on Mr. A. E. Johnson, a retired schoolmaster who was blown away by a gale last November.

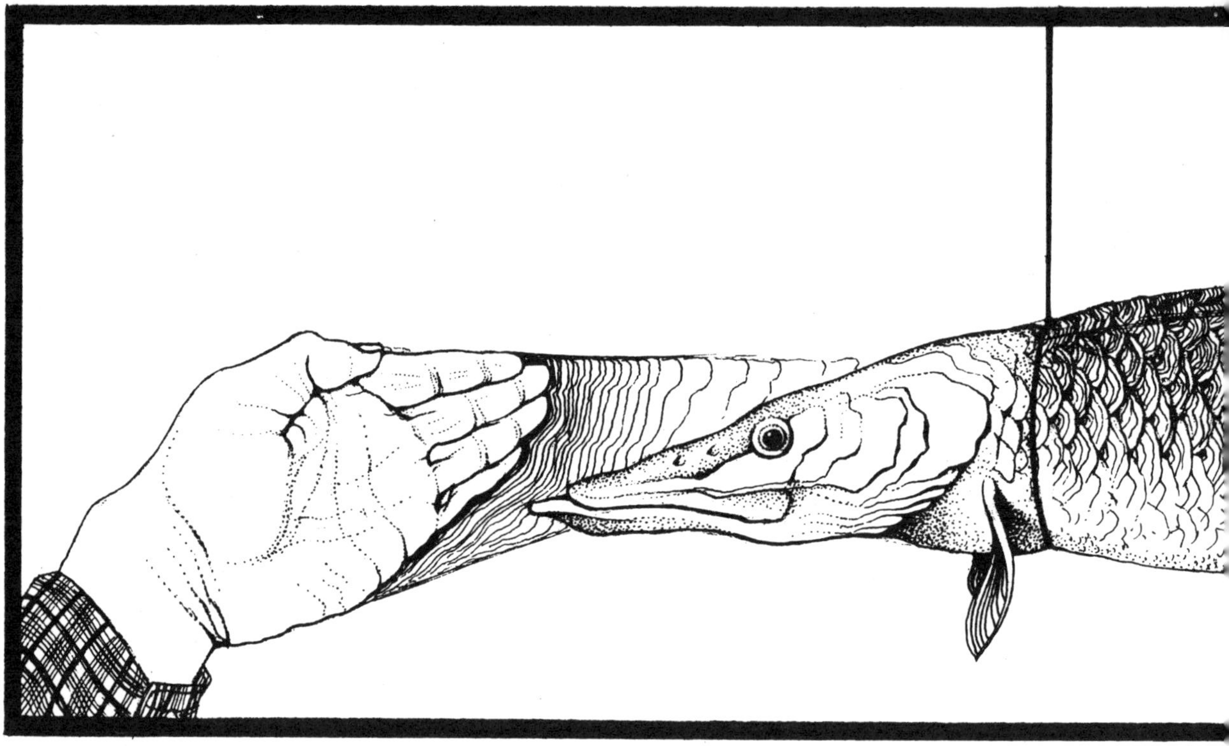

At Angers, France, Mr Robert Expert, landed a 15 lb pike while taking part in an angling contest.

Exclaiming: "This is the biggest catch of my life!" Mr Expert dropped dead in front of his fellow competitors.

"I found that I had acquired a nightmare chip machine," said Mr Christopher Cassap in the course of his evidence against Messrs HFA Marketing Limited.

Placed on the forecourt of his garage, the chip vendor when fed a coin, sometimes emitted one bag of chips, sometimes up to thirty bags. One minute the portions would be stingy, a minute later it was dishing out massive helpings. On other occasions it simply grunted and returned the coin.

Twice the machine boiled over, covering the road with oil.

HFA, claiming £87 arrears of rent against Mr Cassap's claim of £182 worth of wasted chips, said that the machine was designed to dispense Belgian chips.

The Belgian chip, HFA maintained, was thicker than the English chip. Modifications to reduce the chip size to national proportions had been added to the machine at considerable expense. All the machine required was a little patient coaxing.

A Mr Sable of London, supporting Mr Cassap's claim, said that he possessed an identical vendor. It had all the same defects as Mr Cassap's with these refinements: on one occasion his machine served mashed potatoes, and on another, the chips came out completely black.

The case was adjourned.

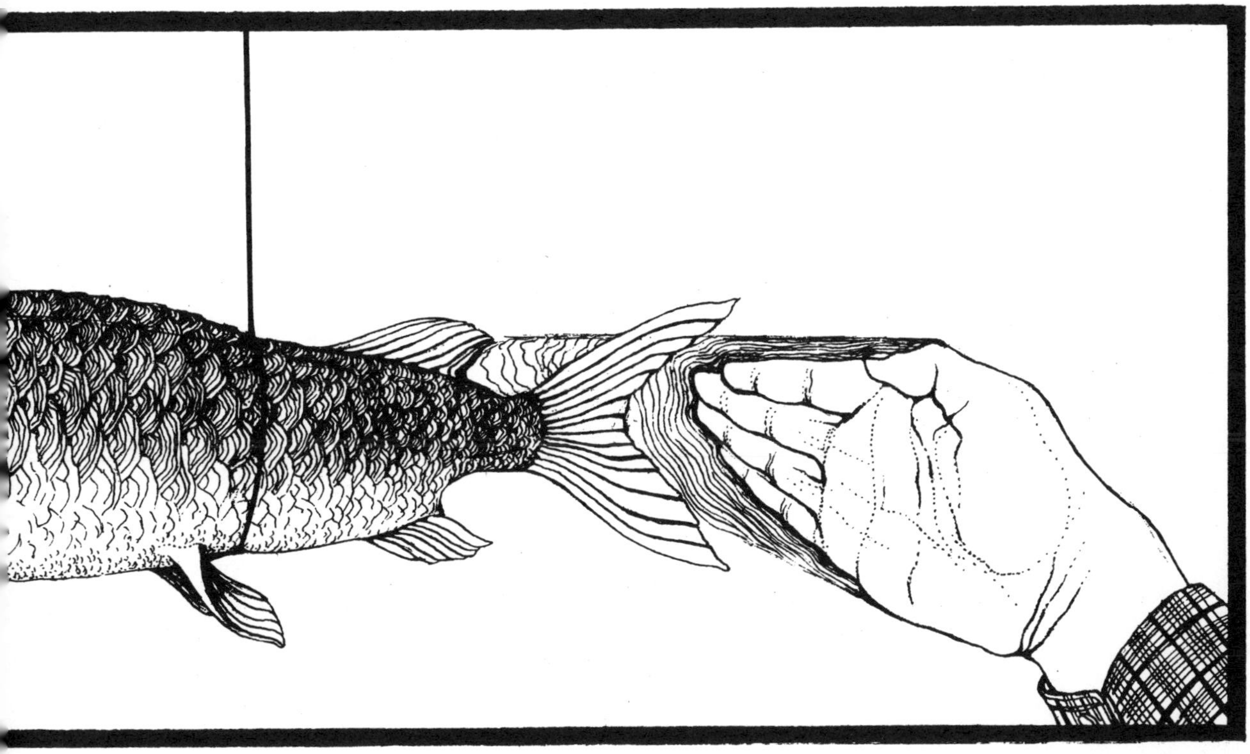

Observing a collie at the wheel of a two-tone Cortina, Police Constable Flynn overtook and flagged it down.

Sitting beside the dog was its owner, Farmer Duff of Drogheda: "Certainly the dog is driving," he said, "its name is Shoo-Shoo, and I took out a license for it after my own was suspended last year."

Later he told the court: "I have driven everything from a plough to a steamroller and I know a good driver when I see one. Shoo-Shoo is up to competition standard."

Emphasising that caution was necessary on the roads, Judge D. Donleavy said: "I once saw a talking horse on the television. It seemed perfectly normal to me. The charge against Farmer Duff is dismissed."

The World Championship Snail Race, held annually at Folkstone, was won by "Festina Lente", a Kentish snail, who won the full distance of 28 inches in 4 minutes 50.8 seconds, defeating last year's winner "Horatio", a Sussex snail, by 9.2 seconds.

Some hours after they were married, Mr Hans Mayer and his bride Elsa retired to the privacy of their bedroom.

Following his bride into their bed, Hans was surprised by her insistence on the following conditions of entry:

1. that he would give to her each week and unopened, his wage packet,
2. that he would pay her, out of what she returned to him by way of spending money, the sum of £5 each time they made love,
3. and that he would never discuss his job, gravedigging, because the subject upset her.

These matters came to light during the trial of Hans for the alleged rape of his wife's young cousin while she was staying with them, and who had been bathing herself in the kitchen at the time of the offence.

Hans explained to the court that after his wife bore their second child she increased her lovemaking fee to £10.

"It was very difficult for me." he said, "I couldn't save enough out of my spending money to pay her. I asked for credit – but she refused to give me any. In nineteen years I could only afford to have her fifteen times. The strain was terrible."

"Why did you marry a woman who imposed such conditions?" the judge asked.

"Before we married everything was free", said Hans.

Elsa confirmed everything her husband had told the court. "Nothing in life is free," she said.

As a measure of revenge for what he considered to be an unjust sentence, Mr Lawrence Patrick Flannagan broke into the Brighton law courts and boiled the Recorder's wig.

Although their doings are comparatively obscure, the world of museum officialdom is no less vainglorious and competitive than that of, say, golfing.

One of the greater London museums acquired what all those who were allowed to see it agreed was a magnificent Graeco-Roman water font, a massive, carven tub of gleaming stone. How things get into museums is often very difficult to say; the governments of underdeveloped, i.e. poor countries have departments that look into such things, museum officialdom stymies these efforts by keeping their acquisitions in the cellar for a considerable time, not more than 50 but seldom less than 25 years.

Anyhow. Shortly after the second world war the museum I have in mind got hold of this font for next to nothing; recently they decided it was safe to put their treasure on show, so, up it came from the glory hold for public delight and edification.

Less than a fortnight after it was put up on display, the curator of the appropriate department received a letter from Albania, the font's place of origin.

Letters from Albania are not all that common in the museum; the curator opened it alone. All it contained was a newspaper clipping bearing a photograph of the font and the headline which read:

FAME FOR LOCAL SCULPTOR

The copy gave details of the sculptor's name, the date of his font, and praised the museum for their good taste.

After 12 years of marriate, Mrs Peter Richardson went to court to give her husband moral support while he answered several charges of burglary.

In the course of the trial she was surprised to hear that the man to whom she believed herself married was, actually, a woman named Miss Rita Daft.

A Russian lady enjoying her leisure on the beach at Ochakov, encircled herself with an inflated tyre before going in. Hardly was she out of her depth when a breeze moved her away from the shore and out into the Black Sea where she floated about for five days.

Last Christmas eve the Tuckers asked the Frys to supper. In the course of the evening Mr Fry gave Mrs Tucker an extravagant kiss under the mistletoe.

This upset Mr Tucker who ran out of the house and threw himself under a passing car.

Seeing his friend lying in the street Mr Fry took an overdose of sleeping pills while Mrs Fry called an ambulance.

When the ambulance arrived – with the police – Mrs Tucker was helping Mr Fry (who had collapsed in the hall) to take more sleeping pills, and Mrs Fry was calling a doctor.

Inspector Callicot tried to take the pills away from Mrs Tucker, who kicked him in the shins for his pains. As Sergeant Courtney Browne went to his Inspector's rescue, Mr Tucker – who had survived the car incident – punched him in the eye for assaulting his wife, while that lady removed her shoe and redoubled her attack on Inspector Callicot.

The ambulance men, excited by the melee, joined in but failed to stop Mrs Tucker driving the Inspector into the bathroom and pushing him into the bath which was filled with vodka.

Mrs Tucker, aged 18, was fined £80.

A young sculptor and his wife were having a quiet evening at home. At about 7.20 pm there was a knock on their door. Answering it, the sculptor found a respectably dressed, middle-aged couple on the step.

"Excuse us," said the woman, "do you have a television?" Before the sculptor could answer the man said: "You see, we don't want to miss Coronation Street and we're a long way from home."

"Sorry," said the sculptor, "we don't have a set." "Never mind " said the woman, "we have ours in the car – can we bring it in?"

This they did, watched the show, and left.

Lack of faith in the workd's banking systems caused Mr Achmed Twfik, a railway linesman of Ufal, near Beirut, to keep his life savings – some £50 – under his mattress.

While he was redecorating the ceiling of his cottage Mr Twfik overreached himself, slipped off the bed, and broke his ankle.

A sheep grazing in a nearby field made its way through the cottage door and, to Mr Twfik's horror, ate his savings that had been spilt over the floor.

Mastering his pain Mr Twfik crawled after the sheep, killed it, removed his money from its stomach, and when he was fit to walk had the notes changed at a bank.

For four years, Mr Sidney Baker, a ticket collector at Folkestone Central said "Good night, Bill," to a particular passenger as he surrendered his ticket and left the platform.

One evening, while Mr Baker was uttering these words the man punched him in the throat, putting him off work for three weeks.

"My name is not Bill, it's Arthur" Mr A. Drake explained to the magistrate. "I got fed up with this Bill business . . . sometimes I used to travel by bus just to avoid it."

After forbidding his sister Constantina, aged 76, to marry her fiance Tantos Diamantopulo, aged 84, Achilles Thistos, aged 86, interrupted their elopement by night. Tantos fell off the ladder and broke his ankle, while Achilles tripped over him and broke his leg.

Constantina is visiting both men in their adjacent hospital beds.

Busts of Tennyson, Dickens, Darwin, Faraday, Gladstone and Disraeli, have been stolen from the front of Stanley Hall, South Norwood.

"They have probably been sold by now," said Mr Smith the hall's manager, "there is a demand for that sort of thing nowadays."

The chief of the Los Angeles Police Mr Edward Davis, has perfected a lightweight portable gallows for punishing hijackers.

"My idea is simple and traditional," said Chief Davis. "We have a moving courtroom in a bus and the gallows is towed behind it in a small trailer. As soon as the criminal is grabbed, we hold a quick trial, find him guilty, and hang him on the main run-way right beneath the observation platform. My gallows has a titanium crossbar and a nylon rope, the trap is fully automatic. All I am waiting for is the re-introduction of the death penalty."

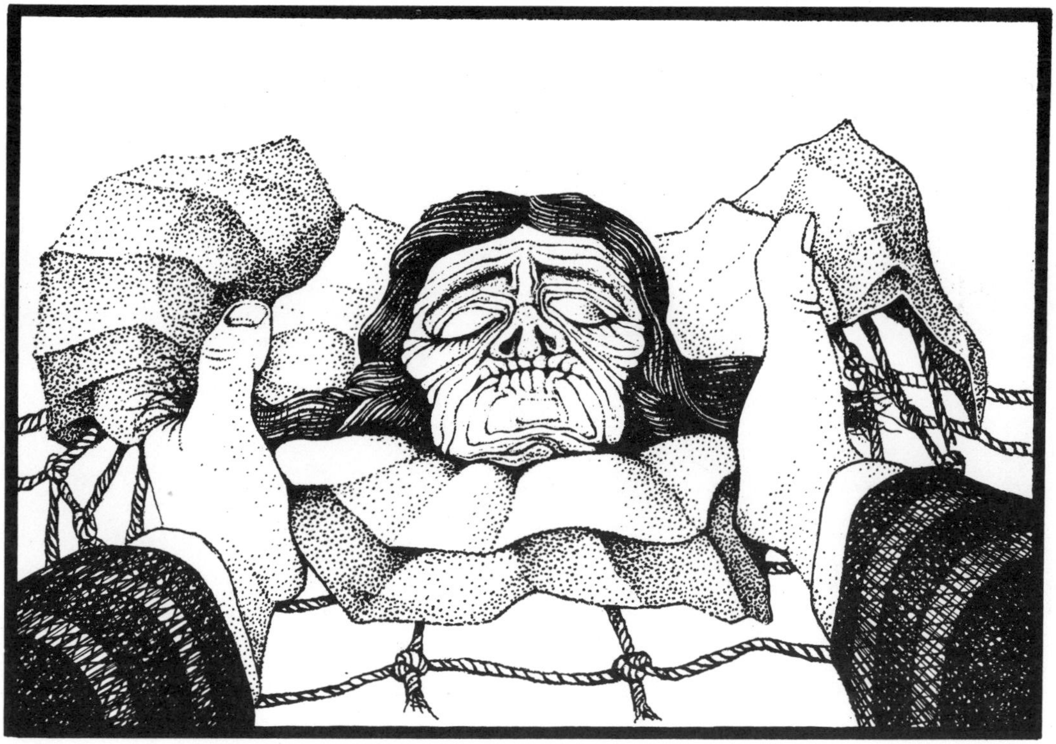

When opened by the appropriate official, a package delivered to the Bordeaux post office from which the label had vanished, was found to contain a human head shrunken to the height of four inches.

Upwards of fifty well-wishers crowded into the ladies lavatory at St Paul's Cray, Kent, to bid farewell to Mrs. Alice Gilbert who is retiring after 45 years as chief attendant.

Alice, known to her regulars as *Mrs. Loo,* handed round drinks, cakes, and sandwiches. The ceremony ended with everyone joining in a chorus of:

"Good-bye, Mrs. Loo,
We're sorry to be leaving you,
Boo-hoo!"

during the closing bars of which all the toilets were flushed in unison.